German
Phrasebook

This edition published 1995 by Brockhampton Press,
a member of Hodder Headline PLC.

ISBN 1 86019 067 7

Printed and bound in Slovenia.

CONTENTS

CONTENTS

KEY TO PRONUNCIATION

Guide to German pronunciation scheme

Vowels

a	as in b<u>a</u>d, f<u>a</u>ther
e	as in b<u>e</u>d, fath<u>e</u>r
ee	as in s<u>ee</u>
i	as in b<u>i</u>t
y	as in b<u>i</u>te
o	as in h<u>o</u>t
oa	as in b<u>oa</u>t
w	as in f<u>ow</u>l
oo	as in p<u>oo</u>l
û	as in French t<u>u</u>

Consonants have approximately the same sounds as in English, but note the following:

g	as in <u>g</u>et
kh	as in the German name Ba<u>ch</u>, Scottish lo<u>ch</u>
zh	as in mea<u>s</u>ure

GETTING STARTED

Everyday words and phrases

Yes
Ja
ya

Please
Bitte
bit-e

Yes, please
Ja bitte
ya bit-e

Thank you
Danke
dank-e

No
Nein
nyn

Excuse me
Entschuldigung
ent-shoold-ee-goong

No, thank you
Nein danke
nyn dank-e

Good
Gut
goot

OK
In Ordnung
in ord-noong

I am very sorry
Es tut mir sehr leid
es toot meer zayr lyt

Being understood

I do not speak German
Ich spreche kein Deutsch
eekh shprekh-e kyn doytsh

I do not understand
Ich verstehe nicht
eekh fer-shtay-e neekht

Being understood

Can you find someone who speaks English?
Könnten Sie jemanden finden, der Englisch spricht?
koent-en zee yay-mand-en find-en der eng-leesh shprikht

Can you help me, please?
Können Sie mir bitte helfen?
koen-en zee meer bit-e help-en

It does not matter
Keine Ursache
kyn-e oor-zakh-e

I do not mind
Macht nichts
makht neekhts

Please repeat that slowly
Bitte wiederholen Sie das langsam
bit-e veed-er-hoal-en zee das lang-zam

Greetings and exchanges

Hello
Hallo
ha-loa

Hi
Hallo
ha-loa

Good evening
Guten Abend
goot-en a-bent

Good morning
Guten Morgen
goot-en mor-gen

Good night
Gute Nacht
goot-e nakht

Goodbye
Auf Wiedersehen
owf veed-er-zay-en

Greetings and exchanges

How are you?
Wie geht es Ihnen?
vee gayt es een-en

I am very well, thank you
Danke, es geht mir sehr gut
dank-e es gayt meer zayr goot

It is good to see you
Schön, Sie zu sehen
shoen zee tsoo zay-en

It is nice to meet you
Angenehm, Ihre Bekanntschaft zu machen
an-ge-naym eer-e be-kannt-shaft tsoo makh-en

There are five of us
Wir sind zu fünft
veer zint tsoo fûnft

Here is my son
Hier ist mein Sohn
heer ist myn zoan

This is — my daughter
Das ist — meine Tochter
das ist —myn-e tokht-er

     — my husband
     — mein Mann
     — myn man

     — my wife
     — meine Frau
     — myn-e frow

Greetings and exchanges

My name is...
Mein Name ist...
*myn **nam**-e ist...*

What is your name?
Was ist Ihr Name?
*vas ist eer **nam**-e*

You are very kind
Sehr nett von Ihnen
*zayr **net** fon **een**-en*

You are very welcome!
Bitte sehr
***bit**-e zayr*

See you soon
Bis bald
*bis **balt***

I am on holiday
Ich bin auf Urlaub
*eekh bin owf **oor**-lowp*

I live in London
Ich wohne in London
*eekh **voan**-e in **lon**-don*

I am a student
Ich bin Student
*eekh bin shtoo-**dent***

I am from America
Ich komme aus Amerika
*eekh **kom**-e ows a-**may**-ree-ka*

Greetings and exchanges

I am from —   Australia
Ich komme aus — Australien
*eekh **kom**-e ows — ow-**stra**-lee-en*

    — Britain
    — Großbritannien
    *— **groas**-bri-**ta**-nee-en*

    — Canada
    — Kanada
    *— **ka**-na-da*

    — England
    — England
    *— **eng**-lant*

    — Ireland
    — Irland
    *— **eer**-lant*

    — New Zealand
    — Neuseeland
    *— noy-**zay**-lant*

    — Scotland
    — Schottland
    *— **shot**-lant*

    — South Africa
    — Südafrika
    *— zûd-**af**-ree-ka*

    — Wales
    — Wales
    *— **wayls***

Common questions

Common questions

Where?	**How?**
Wo?	Wie?
voa	*vee*
Where is...?	**How much?**
Wo ist...?	Wieviel
voa ist	*vee-**feel***
Where are...?	**Who?**
Wo sind...?	Wer?
voa zint	*vayr*
When?	**Why?**
Wann?	Warum?
van	*va-**room***
What?	**Which?**
Was?	Welcher/Welche/Welches
vas	*velkh-er/**velkh**-e/**velkh**-es*

Do you know a good restaurant
Kennen Sie ein gutes Restaurant
ken**-en zee yn **goot**-es rest-oa-**rong

How can I contact American Express/Diners Club?
Wie kann ich mich mit American Express/dem Diners
Club in Verbindung setzen?
***vee** kan eekh meekh mit A-**mer**-ican Express /dem **Dyn**-ers
Club in fer-**bind**-oong **zets**-en*

Common questions

Do you mind if I...
Stört es Sie, wenn ich...
stoert es zee ven eekh...

Have you got any change?
Können Sie wechseln?
koen-en zee veks-eln

How long will it take?
Wie lange dauert das?
vee lang-e dow-ert das

May I borrow your map?
Darf ich Ihre Karte borgen?
darf eekh eer-e kart-e borg-en

What is the problem?
Was ist das Problem
vas ist das prob-laym

What is this?
Was ist das?
vas ist das

What is wrong?
Was ist nicht in Ordnung?
vas ist neekht in ord-noong

What time do you close?
Wann schließen Sie?
van shlees-en zee

Where can I buy a postcard?
Wo kann ich eine Postkarte kaufen?
voa kan eekh yn-e post-kart-e kowf-en

Common questions

Where can I change my clothes?
Wo kann ich mich umziehen?
voa kan eekh meekh oom-tsee-en

Where can we sit down?
Wo können wir uns hinsetzen?
voa koen-en veer oons hin-zets-en

Who did this?
Wer hat das getan?
vayr hat das ge-tan

Who should I see about this?
Mit wem müßte ich darüber sprechen?
mit vaym mûst-e eekh da-rûb-er shprekh-en

Will you come?
Kommen Sie?
kom-en zee

Asking the time

What time is it?
Wieviel Uhr ist es?
vee-feel oor ist es

It is...
Es ist...
es ist ...

a quarter past ten	**a quarter to eleven**
viertel elf	*viertel vor elf/dreiviertel elf*
feer-tel elf	*feer-tel foar elf/dry-veer-tel elf*

Asking the time

after three o'clock
nach drei Uhr
*nakh **dry** oor*

at about one o'clock
etwa um ein Uhr
*et-va oom **yn** oor*

at half past six
um halb sieben
*oom halp **zeeb**-en*

at night
nachts
nakhts

before midnight
vor Mitternacht
*foar **mit**-er-nakht*

early
früh
frû

eleven o'clock
elf Uhr
elf oor

five past ten
fünf nach zehn
*fûnf nakh **tsayn***

five to eleven
fünf vor elf
fûnf foar elf

half past eight exactly
genau halb neun
*ge-**now** halp **noyn***

half past ten
halb elf
*halp **elf***

in an hour's time
in einer Stunde
*in yn-er **shtoond**-e*

in half an hour
in einer halben Stunde
*in yn-er halb-en **shtoond**-e*

late
spät
spet

midnight
Mitternacht
***mit**-er-nakht*

nearly five o'clock
fast fünf Uhr
*fast **fûnf** oor*

soon
bald
balt

ten o' clock
zehn Uhr
***tsayn** oor*

Asking the time

ten past ten
zehn nach zehn
tsayn nakh tsayn

ten to eleven
zehn vor elf
tsayn foar elf

this afternoon
heute Nachmittag
hoyt-e nakh-mi-tag

this evening
heute Abend
hoyt-e a-bent

this morning
heute morgen
hoyt-e mor-gen

tonight
heute nacht
hoyt-e nakht

twelve o'clock (midday)
zwölf Uhr (Mittag)
tsvoelf oor (mi-tag)

twenty five past ten
fünfundzwanzig Minuten
nach zehn
fûnf-oont-tsvan-tseekh mee-noo-ten nakh tsayn

twenty five to eleven
fünfundzwanzig Minuten
vor elf
fûnf-oont-tsvan-tseekh mee-noo-ten voar elf

twenty past ten
zwanzig Minuten nach
zehn
tsvan-tseekh mee-noo-ten nakh tsayn

twenty to eleven
zwanzig Minuten vor elf
tsvan-tseekh mee-noo-ten foar elf

two hours ago
vor zwei Stunden
foar tsvy shtoond-en

Common problems

I am late
Ich bin schon zu spät
*eekh bin **shoan** tsoo **shpet***

I have dropped a contact lens
Mir ist eine Kontaktlinse heruntergefallen
***meer** ist yn-e kon-**takt**-linz-e hayr-**oont**-er-ge-fal-en*

I have no currency
Ich habe nicht die richtige Währung
*eekh **hab**-e neekht dee **reekht**-eeg-e **ver**-oong*

I haven't enough money
Ich habe nicht genug Geld
*eekh **hab**-e neekht ge-**noog** gelt*

I have lost my — credit cards
Ich habe meine — Kreditkarten verloren
*eekh **hab**-e myn-e —kray-**deet**-kart-en fer-**loar**-en*

— key
— Schlüssel verloren
*—**shlûs**-el fer-**loar**-en*

— ticket
— Karte verloren
*—**kart**-e fer-**loar**-en*

— traveller's cheques
— Reiseschecks verloren
*—**ryz**-e-sheks fer-**loar**-en*

Common problems

My car has been stolen
Mein Wagen wurde gestohlen
*myn **vag**-en voord-e ge-**shtoal**-en*

My handbag has been stolen
Meine Handtasche wurde gestohlen
*myn-e **hant**-tash-e voord-e ge-**shtoal**-en*

My wallet has been stolen
Mein Geldbeutel wurde gestohlen
*myn **gelt**-boyt-el voord-e ge-**shtoal**-en*

My son is lost
Ich habe meinen Sohn verloren
*eekh **hab**-e myn-en **zoan** fer-**loar**-en*

Arrival

Here is my passport
Da ist mein Paß
da ist myn pas

I am attending a convention
Ich wohne einer Versammlung bei
eekh voan-e yn-er fer-zam-loong by

I am here on business
Ich bin geschäftlich hier
eekh bin ge-sheft-leekh heer

I will be staying here for eight weeks
Ich bleibe acht Wochen lang hier
eekh blyb-e akht vokh-en lang heer

We are visiting friends
Wir besuchen Freunde
veer be-zookh-en froynd-e

We have a joint passport
Wir haben einen Sammelpaß
veer hab-en yn-en zam-el-pas

I have nothing to declare
Ich habe nichts anzumelden
eekh hab-e neekhts an-tsoo-meld-en

I have the usual allowances
Ich habe die üblichen zollfrei erlaubten Mengen
eekh hab-e dee ûb-leekh-en tsol-fry er-lowp-ten meng-en

Arrival

How long will this take?
Wie lange dauert das?
*vee **lang**-e **dow**-ert das*

How much do I have to pay?
Was habe ich zu zahlen?
*vas hab-e eekh tsoo **tsal**-en*

This is for my own use
Das ist für meinen eigenen Gebrauch
das** ist fûr myn-en **yg**-en-en ge-**browkh

Common probems and requests

Can I upgrade to first class?
Kann ich ein Upgrade zur ersten Klasse haben?
***kan** eekh yn **up**-grayd tsoor **erst**-en klas-e **hab**-en*

How long will the delay be?
Wie groß ist die Verspätung?
*vee **groas** ist dee fer-**spet**-oong*

I am in a hurry
Ich bin in Eile
*eekh bin in **yl**-e*

I have lost my ticket
Ich habe mein Ticket verloren
*eekh **hab**-e myn tik-et fer-**loar**-en*

I have missed my connection
Ich habe meinen Anschluß verpaßt
*eekh **hab**-e myn-en **an**-shloos fer-**past***

Common problems and requests

The people who were to meet me have not arrived
Die Leute, die mich abholen sollten, sind nicht angekommen
dee loyt-e dee meekh ap-hoal-en zolt-en zint neekht an-ge-kom-en

Where is the toilet?
Wo finde ich eine Toilette?
voa find-e eekh eyn-e toy-let-e

Where is — the bar?
   Wo ist — die Bar?
   voa ist — dee bar

            — the information desk?
            — der Informationsschalter?
            — der in-for-ma-tsee-oans-shalt-er

            — the departure lounge?
            — der Wartesaal?
            — voa ist der vart-e-zal

            — the transfer desk?
            — der Transfer-Schalter
            — der trans-fer-shalt-er

Where can I buy currency?
Wo kann ich Landeswährung kaufen?
voa kan eekh land-ez-ver-oong kowf-en

Where can I change traveller's cheques?
Wo kann ich meine Reiseschecks umwechseln?
voa kan eekh myn-e ryz-e-sheks oom-veks-eln

Where can I get a taxi?
Wo kann ich ein Taxi nehmen?
voa kan eekh yn tax-ee naym-en

Common problems and requests

Where do I get the connection flight to Cologne?
Wo finde ich einen Anschlußflug nach Köln?
voa find-e eekh yn-en an-shloos-floog nakh koeln

Where will I find the airline representative?
Wo finde ich einen Vertreter der Fluggesellschaft?
voa find-e eekh yn-en fer-trayt-er der floog-ge-zel-shaft

My flight was late
Mein Flug hat sich verspätet
myn floog hat zeekh fer-shpet-et

I was delayed at the airport
Ich wurde am Flughafen aufgehalten
eekh woord-e am floog-haf-en owf-ge-halt-en

I was held up at immigration
Ich wurde bei den Einwanderungsbehörden aufgehalten
eekh woord-e by den yn-vand-er-oongs-be-hoerd-en owf-gehalt-en

Luggage

Where is the baggage from flight number...?
Wo ist das Gepäck von Flug Nummer...?
voa ist das ge-pek fon floog noom-er...

Are there any baggage trolleys?
Gibt es hier Gepäckwagen?
gipt es heer ge-pek-vag-en

Can I have help with my bag?
Könnte mir jemand mit meiner Tasche helfen?
koent-e meer yay-mant mit myn-er tash-e helf-en

Luggage

Careful, the handle is broken
Achtung, der Griff ist kaputt
akh-toong der grif ist ka-poot

I will carry that myself
Das trage ich selbst
das trag-e eekh zelpst

Is there a left-luggage office?
Gibt es hier eine Gepäckverwarung?
gipt es heer yn-e ge-pek-fer-var-oong

Is there any charge?
Kostet das etwas?
kost-et das et-vas

Where is my bag?
Wo ist meine Tasche?
voa ist myn-e tash-e

I have lost my bag
Ich habe meine Tasche verloren
eekh **hab**-e myn-e **tash**-e fer-**loar**-en

It is — a large suitcase
Es ist — ein großer Koffer
es ist —yn gros-er kof-er

> **— a rucksack**
> — ein Rucksack
> *—yn rook-zak*

> **— a small bag**
> — eine kleine Tasche
> *—yn-e klyn-e tash-e*

Luggage

My baggage has not arrived
Mein Gepäck ist nicht angekommen
myn ge-pek ist neekht an-ge-kom-en

Please take these bags to a taxi
Bitte bringen Sie diese Taschen in ein Taxi
bit-e bring-en zee deez-e tash-en in yn tax-ee

These bags are not mine
Das ist nicht mein Gepäck
das ist neekht myn ge-pek

This package is fragile
Dieses Paket ist zerbrechlich
deez-es pa-kayt ist tser-brekh-leekh

No, do not put that on top
Nein, stellen Sie das bitte nicht darauf
nyn shtel-en zee das bit-e neekht da-rowf

At the Hotel

Reservations and enquiries

I am sorry I am late
Bitte entschuldigen Sie die Verspätung
bit-e ent-shoold-eeg-en zee dee fer-shpet-oong

I have a reservation
Ich habe gebucht
eekh hab-e ge-bookht

I shall be staying until July 4th
Ich werde bis vierten Juli bleiben
eekh vayrd-e bis feer-ten yool-ee blyb-en

I want to stay for 5 nights
Ich möchte fünfmal übernachten
eekh moekht-e fûnf-mal û-ber-nakht-en

Do you have a double room with a bath?
Haben Sie ein Doppelzimmer mit Bad?
hab-en zee yn dop-el-tsim-er mit bat

Do you have a room with twin beds and a shower?
Haben Sie ein Zweibettzimmer mit Dusche?
hab-en zee yn svy-bet-tsim-er mit doosh-e

Do you have a single room?
Haben Sie ein Einzelzimmer?
hab-en zee yn yn-tsel-tsim-er

I need a double room with a bed for a child
Ich brauche ein Doppelzimmer mit Kinderbett
eekh browkh-e yn dop-el-tsim-er mit kind-er-bet

Reservations and enquiries

I need — a single room with a shower or bath
Ich brauche — ein Einzelzimmer mit Dusche oder Bad
eekh browkh-e — yn yn-tsel-tsim-er mit doosh-e oad-er bat

— a room with a double bed
— ein Doppelzimmer
— yn dop-el-tsim-er

— a room with twin beds and bath
— ein Zweibettzimmer mit Bad
— yn tsvy-bet-tsim-er mit bat

— a single room
— ein Einzelzimmer
— yn yn-tsel-stim-er

How much is — full board?
Wieviel kostet — Vollpension?
vee-feel kost-et — fol-pen-see-oan

— half-board?
— Halbpension?
— halp-pen-see-oan

— it per night?
— es pro Nacht?
— es pro nakht

— the room per night?
— das Zimmer pro Nacht?
— das tsim-er pro nakht

Do you take traveller's cheques?
Nehmen Sie Reiseschecks?
naym-en zee ryz-e-sheks

Reservations and enquiries

Does the price include— room and breakfast?
Beinhaltet der Preis— Übernachtung und Frühstück
*be-**in**-halt-et der **prys**— **ûb**-er-nakht-oong oont **frû**-shtook*

— room and all meals?
— Übernachtung und alle Mahlzeiten
— ***ûb**-er-nakht-oong oont al-e **mal**-tsyt-en*

— room and dinner?
— Übernachtung und Abendessen
— ***ûb**-ernakht-oong ont **ab**-ent-es-en*

Can we have adjoining rooms?
Könnten wir Zimmer nebeneinander haben?
***koent**-en veer **tsim**-er nay-ben-yn-**and**-er **hab**-en*

Do you have a car park?
Haben Sie einen Gästeparkplatz?
***hab**-en zee yn-en **gest**-e-park-plats*

Do you have a cot for my baby?
Haben Sie ein Kinderbett für mein Baby?
***hab**-en zee yn **kind**-er-bet fûr myn **bayb**-ee*

Are there supervised activities for the children?
Gibt es beaufsichtigte Aktivitäten für Kinder?
***gipt** es be-**owf**-zeekht-eegt-e ak-teev-ee-**tet**-en fûr **kind**-er*

Can my son sleep in our room?
Kann mein Sohn in unserem Zimmer schlafen?
***kan** myn **zoan** in oonz-er-em **tsim**-er shlaf-en*

Are there other children staying at the hotel?
Wohnen noch andere Kinder in diesem Hotel?
voan**-en nokh **and**-er-e **kind**-er in **deez**-em hoa-**tel

Reservations and enquiries

Do you have a fax machine?
Haben Sie ein Faxgerät?
*hab-en zee yn **fax**-ge-ret*

Do you have a laundry service?
Haben Sie einen Waschdienst?
*hab-en zee yn-en **vash**-deenst*

Do you have a safe for valuables?
Haben Sie einen Safe für Wertsachen?
*hab-en zee yn-en **sayf** fûr **vert**-zakh-en*

Do you have any English newspapers?
Haben Sie englische Zeitungen?
*hab-en zee **eng**-leesh-e **tsyt**-oong-en*

Do you have satellite TV?
Haben Sie Satellitenfernsehen?
hab-en zee za-te-**leet**-en-**fern**-zay-en

Which floor is my room on?
Auf welchem Stock ist mein Zimmer?
*owf **velkh**-em shtok ist myn **tsim**-er*

Is there a casino?
Gibt es hier ein Kasino?
*gipt es **heer** yn ka-**see**-noa*

Is there a hairdryer?
Gibt es einen Föhn?
*gipt es yn-en **foen***

Is there a lift?
Haben Sie einen Aufzug?
*hab-en zee yn-en **owf**-tsoog*

Reservations and enquiries

Is there a minibar?
Gibt es eine Minibar?
gipt es yn-e meen-ee-bar

Is there a sauna?
Haben Sie eine Sauna?
hab-en zee yn-e zown-a

Is there a swimming pool?
Haben Sie ein Schwimmbecken?
hab-en zee yn shvim-bek-en

Is there a telephone?
Gibt es ein Telefon?
gipt es yn tay-lay-foan

Is there a television?
Gibt es ein Fernsehgerät?
gipt es yn fern-zay-ge-ret

Is there a trouser press?
Gibt es eine Hosenpresse?
gipt es yn-e hoaz-en-pres-e

What is the voltage here?
Wie hoch ist die Spannung hier?
vee hoakh ist dee shpan-oong heer

Is the voltage 220 or 110?
Beträgt die Spannung 220 oder 110 Volt?
*be-tregt dee shpan-oong tsvy-hoond-ert-tsvan-tseekh oad-er
hoond-ert-tsayn volt*

Is this a safe area?
Ist das eine sichere Gegend?
ist das yn-e zeekh-er-e gay-gent

Reservations and enquiries

Is there a market in the town?
Gibt es in dieser Stadt einen Markt?
*gipt es in deez-er **shtat** yn-en **markt***

Can you recommend a good local restaurant?
Können Sie ein gutes Restaurant in der Nähe empfehlen?
*koen-en zee yn **goot**-es rest-oa-**rong** in der **ne**-e emp-**fayl**-en*

Is there a Chinese restaurant?
Gibt es hier ein chinesisches Lokal?
*gipt es **heer** yn khee-**nayz**-eesh-es loa-**kal***

Is there an Indian restaurant?
Gibt es hier ein indisches Lokal?
*gipt es **heer** yn **in**-deesh-es loa-**kal***

Can I use traveller's cheques?
Kann ich mit Reiseschecks zahlen?
*kan eekh mit **ryz**-e-sheks **tsal**-en*

Has my colleague arrived yet?
Ist mein Kollege schon angekommen?
*ist myn ko-**layg**-e shoan **an**-ge-kom-en*

What time does the restaurant close?
Wann schließt das Restaurant?
*van **shleest** das rest-oa-**rong***

When does the bar open?
Wann öffnet die Bar?
*van **oef**-net dee **bar***

What time does the hotel close?
Wann schließt das Hotel?
*van **shleest** das hoa-**tel***

Service

What time is — breakfast?
Wann wird das — Frühstück — serviert?
van virt das —frû-shtûk —zer-veert

> **— dinner?**
> — das Abendessen?
> —*das a-bent-es-en*

> **— lunch?**
> — das Mittagessen?
> —*das mi-tag-es-en*

Service

Can I make a telephone call from here?
Kann ich von hier aus telefonieren?
kan eekh fon heer ows tay-lay-fo-neer-en

Can I dial direct from my room?
Kann ich von meinem Zimmer aus direkt wählen?
kan eekh fon myn-em tsim-er ows dee-rekt vel-en

Can I have an outside line?
Könnte ich eine Verbindung nach draußen haben?
koent-e eekh yn-e fer-bind-oong nakh drows-en hab-en

Can I charge this to my room?
Kann ich das auf meine Rechnung setzen lassen?
kan eekh das owf myn-e rekh-noong zets-en las-en

Can I have my key, please?
Kann ich bitte meinen Schlüssel haben?
kan eekh bit-e myn-en shlûs-el hab-en

Service

Can I have — a newspaper?
   Kann ich — eine Zeitung haben?
   *kan eekh — yn-e **tsyt**-oong hab-en*

       — an ashtray?
       — einen Aschenbecher?
       *—yn-en **ash**-en-bekh-er*

       — another blanket?
       — noch eine Decke?
       *—**nokh** yn-e **dek**-e*

       — another pillow?
       — noch ein Kissen?
       *—**nokh** yn **kis**-en*

Can I have my wallet from the safe?
Könnten Sie mir bitte meine Brieftasche aus dem Safe geben?
*koent-en zee meer **bit**-e myn-e **breef**-tash-e ows dem **sayf** **gayb**-en*

Can I hire a portable telephone?
Kann ich ein tragbares Telefon mieten?
*kan eekh yn **trag**-bar-es tay-lay-**foan** meet-en*

Can I send this by courier?
Kann ich das per Kurier schicken?
*kan eekh das per koo-**reer** shik-en*

Can I use my charge card?
Kann ich meine Kundenkreditkarte verwenden?
*kan eekh myn-e **koond**-en kray-**deet**-kart-e fer-**vend**-en*

Service

Can I use my personal computer here?
Kann ich meinen Computer hier verwenden?
kan eekh myn-en com-pyoot-er heer fer-vend-en

Can we have breakfast in our room, please?
Können wir bitte in unserem Zimmer frühstücken?
koen-en veer bit-e in oons-er-em tsim-er frû-shtûk-en

Is there a room service menu?
Gibt es eine Karte für den Zimmerservice?
gipt es yn-e kart-e fûr den tsim-er-zer-vees

I need an early morning call
Ich möchte morgen früh geweckt werden
eekh moekht-e mor-gen frû ge-vekt vayrd-en

Is there a trouser press I can use?
Gibt es eine Hosenpresse, die ich verwenden kann?
gipt es yn-e hoaz-en-pres-e dee eekh fer-vend-en kan

I am expecting a fax
Ich erwarte ein Fax
eekh er-vart-e yn fax

Where can I send a fax?
Wo kann ich ein Fax senden?
voa kan eekh yn fax send-en

I need to charge these batteries
Ich muß diese Batterien aufladen
eekh moos deez-e bat-er-ee-en owf-lad-en

I want to press these clothes
Ich möchte meine Kleider bügeln
eekh moekht-e myn-e klyd-er bûg-eln

Service

Please can I leave a message?
Kann ich bitte eine Nachricht hinterlassen?
*kan eekh bit-e yn-e **nakh**-reekht **hint**-er-las-en*

My room number is 22
Meine Zimmernummer ist 22
*myn-e **tsim**-er-noom-er ist tsvy-oont-**tsvan**-tseekh*

Please fill the minibar
Würden Sie bitte die Minibar wieder auffüllen?
*vûrd-en zee **bit**-e dee **meen**-ee-bar veed-er **owf**-fûl-en*

       I need — a razor
   Ich brauche — einen Rasierapparat
*eekh **browkh**-e —yn-en ra-**zeer**-a-pa-rat*

               — some soap
               — Seife
               *—**zyf**-e*

               — some toilet paper
               — Toilettenpapier
               *—toy-**let**-en-pa-**peer***

               — some towels
               — Handtücher
               *—**hant**-tûkh-er*

               — some coat hangers
               — ein paar Bügel
               *—yn par **bûg**-el*

               — some note paper
               — etwas Schreibpapier
               *—et-vas **shryb**-pa-**peer***

Problems

Please turn the heating off
Würden Sie bitte die Heizung abschalten?
vûrd-en zee bit-e dee hyts-oong ap-shalt-en

Please, wake me at 7 o'clock in the morning
Wecken Sie mich bitte um 7 Uhr.
vek-en zee meekh bit-e oom zeeb-en oor

Please send this fax for me
Bitte senden Sie dieses Fax für mich
bit-e zend-en zee deez-es fax fûr meekh

Where is the manager?
Wo ist der Manager?
voa ist der man-a-ger

Can I speak to the manager?
Kann ich mit dem Manager sprechen?
kan eekh mit dem man-a-ger shprekh-en

Hello, this is the manager
Guten Tag, hier spricht der Direktor
goot-en tag heer sprikht der di-rek-tor

Problems

I cannot close the window
Ich kann das Fenster nicht schließen
eekh kan das fenst-er neekht shlees-en

I cannot open the window
Ich kann das Fenster nicht öffnen
eekh kan das fenst-er neekht oef-nen

Problems

The air conditioning is not working
Die Klimaanlage funktioniert nicht
*dee **kleem**-a-an-lag-e foonk-tsee-o-**neert** neekht*

The bathroom is dirty
Das Badezimmer ist schmutzig
*das **bad**-e-tsim-er ist **shmootz**-eekh*

The heating is not working
Die Heizung funktioniert nicht
*dee **hyts**-oong foonk-tsee-o-**neert** neekht*

The light is not working
Das Licht funktioniert nicht
*das **leekht** foonk-tsee-o-**neert** neekht*

The room is not serviced
Für dieses Zimmer besteht kein Zimmerservice
*für dees-es **tsim**-er be-shtayt kyn **tsim**-er-**ser**-vees*

The room is too noisy
Das Zimmer ist zu laut
*das **tsim**-er ist tsoo **lowt***

The room key does not work
Der Zimmerschlüssel sperrt nicht
*der **tsim**-er-shlûs-el **spert** neekht*

There are no towels in the room
In dem Zimmer sind keine Handtücher
*in dem **tsim**-er zint kyn-e **hant**-tûkh-er*

There is no hot water
Wir haben kein heißes Wasser
*veer **hab**-en kyn **hys**-es **vas**-er*

There is no plug for the washbasin
Im Waschbecken ist kein Stöpsel
*im **vash**-bek-en ist kyn **shtoep**-sel*

Checking out

We will be leaving early tomorrow
Wir werden morgen früh abfahren
*veer vayrd-en **morg**-en frû **ap**-far-en*

I have to leave tomorrow
Ich muß morgen wegfahren
*eekh moos **morg**-en **vayg**-far-en*

Can I have the bill please?
Kann ich bitte die Rechnung haben?
*kan eekh bit-e dee **rekh**-noong hab-en*

I want to stay an extra night
Ich möchte eine Nacht länger bleiben
*eekh **moekht**-e yn-e **nakht** leng-er **blyb**-en*

Do I have to change rooms?
Muß ich in ein anderes Zimmer ziehen?
*moos eekh in yn **and**-er-es **tsim**-er **tsee**-en*

Could you have my bags brought down?
Könnten Sie mein Gepäck bitte herunterbringen lassen?
*koent-en zee myn ge-**pek** bit-e hayr-**oont**-er-**bring**-en **las**-en*

Please leave the bags in the lobby
Lassen Sie das Gepäck bitte in der Eingangshalle stehen
*las-en zee das ge-**pek** bit-e in der **yn**-gangs-hal-e **shtay**-en*

Checking out

Could you order me a taxi?
Könnten Sie bitte ein Taxi rufen?
koent-en zee bit-e yn tax-ee roof-en

Thank you, we enjoyed our stay
Vielen Dank, wir hatten einen sehr angenehmen
Aufenthalt
*feel-en dank veer hat-en yn-en zayk an-gen-naym-en
owf-ent-halt*

OTHER ACCOMODATION

Renting a house

We have rented this villa
Wir haben dieses Ferienhaus gemietet
*veer **hab**-en deez-es **fayr**-i-en-hows ge-**meet**-et*

Here is our booking form
Hier ist unser Buchungsformular
heer ist unz-er **bookh**-oongs-form-oo-**lar**

We need two sets of keys
Wir brauchen die Schlüssel in zweifacher Ausführung
*veer **browkh**-en dee **shlûs**-el in **tsvy**-fakh-er ows-**fûr**-oong*

When does the cleaner come?
Wann kommt die Putzfrau?
*van komt dee **poots**-frow*

Where is the bathroom?
Wo ist das Badezimmer?
*voa ist das **bad**-e-tsim-er*

Can I contact you on this number?
Kann ich Sie unter dieser Nummer erreichen?
***kan** eekh zee **oont**-er deez-er **noom**-er er-**rykh**-en*

Can you send a repairman?
Können Sie jemanden zum Reparieren schicken?
***koen**-en zee **jaym**-an-den tsoom re-pa-**reer**-en **shik**-en*

How does this work?
Wie funktioniert das?
*vee foonk-tsee-o-**neert** das*

Renting a house

I cannot open the shutters
Ich kann die Fensterläden nicht öffnen
*eekh kan dee **fenst-er-led**-en neekht **oef**-nen*

Is the water heater working?
Funktioniert der Warmwasserbereiter
*foonk-tsee-o-**neert** der **varm**-vas-er-be-**ry**-ter*

Is the water safe to drink?
Kann man das Wasser unbedenklich trinken?
*kan man das **vas**-er **oon**-be-denk-leekh **trink**-en*

Is there any spare bedding?
Gibt es zusätzliches Bettzeug?
*gipt es **tsoo**-zets-leekh-es **bet**-tsoyg*

The cooker does not work
Der Herd funktioniert nicht
*der **hert** foonk-tsee-o-**neert** neekht*

The refrigerator does not work
Der Kühlschrank funktioniert nicht
*der **kûl**-shrank foonk-tsee-o-**neert** neekht*

The toilet is blocked
Die Toilette ist verstopft
*dee toy-**let**-e ist fer-**shtopft***

There is a leak
Da ist eine undichte Stelle
*da ist yn-e **oon**-deekht-e **shtel**-e*

We do not have any water
Wir haben kein Wasser
*veer **hab**-en kyn **vas**-er*

Around the house

Where is the fuse box?
Wo ist der Sicherungskasten?
voa ist der zeekh-er-oongs-kast-en

Where is the key for this door?
Wo ist der Schlüssel für diese Tür?
voa ist der shlûs-el fûr deez-e tur

Where is the socket for my razor?
Wo ist die Steckdose für meinen Rasierapparat?
voa ist dee shtek-doz-e fûr myn-en ra-zeer-ap-a-rat

Around the house

bath Bad *bat*	**chair** Stuhl *shtool*
bathroom Badezimmer *bad-e-tsim-er*	**cooker** Herd *hert*
bed Bett *bet*	**corkscrew** Korkenzieher *kork-en-tsee-er*
brush Bürste *bûrst-e*	**cup** Tasse *tas-e*
can opener Dosenöffner *doaz-en-oef-ner*	**fork** Gabel *gab-el*

Around the house

glass
Glas
glas

kitchen
Küche
kûkh-e

knife
Messer
mes-er

mirror
Spiegel
shpeeg-el

pan
Pfanne
pfan-e

plate
Teller
tel-er

refrigerator
Kühlschrank
kûl-shrank

sheet
Bettuch
bet-tookh

sink
Spüle
shpû-le

spoon
Löffel
loef-el

stove
Ofen
oa-fen

table
Tisch
tish

tap
Wasserhahn
was-er-han

toilet
Toilette
toy-let-e

vacuum cleaner
Staubsauger
shtowp-zowg-er

washbasin
Waschbecken
vash-bek-en

Camping

Can we camp in your field?
Können wir auf Ihrem Feld zelten?
koen-en veer owf eer-em felt tselt-en

Can we camp near here?
Können wir hier in der Nähe zelten?
koen-en veer heer in der ne-e tselt-en

Can we park our caravan here?
Können wir unseren Caravan hier parken?
koen-en veer oons-er-en ka-ra-van heer park-en

Do I pay in advance?
Zahle ich im voraus?
tsal-e eekh im foar-ows

Do I pay when I leave?
Zahle ich bei der Abreise?
tsal-e eekh by der ap-ryz-e

Is there a more sheltered site?
Gibt es einen geschützteren Platz?
gipt es yn-en ge-shûts-ter-en plats

Is there a restaurant or a shop on the site?
Gibt es auf dem Platz ein Restaurant oder einen Laden?
gipt es owf dem plats yn rest-o-rong od-er yn-en lad-en

Is there another campsite near there?
Gibt es einen anderen Campingplatz in der Nähe?
gipt es yn-en and-er-en kamp-ing-plats in der ne-e

Camping

Is this the drinking water?
Ist das Trinkwasser?
*ist das **trink**-vas-er*

Please can we pitch our tent here?
Können wir bitte unser Zelt hier aufstellen?
***koen**-en veer **bit**-e oons-er **tselt** heer **owf**-shtel-en*

The site is very wet and muddy
Das Gelände ist sehr naß und schlammig
*das ge-**lend**-e ist zayr **nas** oont **shlam**-eekh*

Where are the toilets?
Wo sind die Toiletten?
***voa** zint dee toy-**let**-en*

Where can I have a shower?
Wo kann ich mich duschen?
***voa** kan eekh meekh **doosh**-en*

Where can we wash our dishes?
Wo kann ich unser Geschirr abspülen?
***voa** kan eekh oons-er ge-**shir** ap-shpûl-en*

Around the campsite

Air mattress Luftmatratze *looft-ma-trats-e*	**bucket** Eimer *ym-er*
bottle-opener Flaschenöffner *flash-en-oef-ner*	**camp bed** Feldbett *felt-bet*

Around the campsite

camp chair
Klappstuhl
klap-shtool

can-opener
Dosenöffner
doz-en-oef-ner

candle
Kerze
kerts-e

cup
Tasse
tas-e

fire
Feuer
foy-er

fly sheet
Fliegennetz
fleeg-en-nets

fork
Gabel
gab-el

frying pan
Bratpfanne
brat-pfan-e

ground sheet
Bodenabdeckung
boad-en-ap-dek-oong

guy line
Zeltleine
tselt-lyn-e

knife
Messer
mes-er

mallet
Holzhammer
holts-ham-er

matches
Streichhölzer
shtrykh-hoelts-er

penknife
Taschenmesser
tash-en-mes-er

plate
Teller
tel-er

rucksack
Rucksack
rook-zak

sleeping bag
Schlafsack
shlaf-zak

spoon
Löffel
loef-el

Around the campsite

stove Ofen *oaf-en*	**tent** Zelt *tselt*
tent peg Hering *hayr-ing*	**thermos flask** Thermosflasche *ter-moas-flash-e*
tent pole Zeltstange *tselt-shtang-e*	**torch** Taschenlampe *tash-en-lamp-e*

Hostelling

Are you open during the day?
Sind Sie tagsüber geöffnet?
zint zee tags-ûb-er ge-oef-net

Can I join here?
Können wir hier Mitglied werden?
koen-en veer heer mit-gleet vayrd-en

Can I use the kitchen?
Kann ich die Küche benutzen?
kan eekh dee kûkh-e be-noots-en

Can we stay five nights here?
Können wir fünf Nächte hier bleiben?
koen-en veer fûnf nekht-e heer blyb-en

Can we stay until Sunday?
Können wir bis Sonntag bleiben?
koen-en veer bis zon-tag blyb-en

Do you serve meals?
Servieren Sie auch Mahlzeiten?
*ser-**veer**-en zee owkh **mal**-tsyt-en*

— to take away?
— zum Mitnehmen?
*— tsoom **mit**-naym-en*

Here is my membership card
Hier ist meine Mitgliedschaftskarte
*heer ist myn-e **mit**-gleet-shafts-**kart**-e*

I do not have my card
Ich habe meine Karte nicht
*eekh **hab**-e myn-e **kart**-e neekht*

Is there a youth hostel near here?
Gibt es eine Jugendherberge in der Nähe?
*gipt es yn-e **yoog**-ent-hayr-berg-e in der **ne**-e*

What time do you close?
Wann schließen Sie?
*van **shlees**-en zee*

Childcare

Can you warm this milk for me?
Können Sie mir diese Milch aufwärmen?
*koen-en zee meer deez-e **milkh** owf-verm-en*

Do you have a high chair?
Haben Sie einen Hochstuhl?
*hab-en zee yn-en **hoakh**-shtool*

Childcare

How old is your daughter?
Wie alt ist Ihre Tochter?
*vee **alt** ist eer-e **tokht**-er*

I am very sorry. That was very naughty of him
Tut mir sehr leid. Das war sehr böse von ihm.
***toot** meer zayr **lyt** das var zayr **boez**-e fon eem*

Is there a baby-sitter?
Haben Sie einen Babysitter?
***hab**-en zee yn-en **bayb**-ee-sit-er*

Is there a cot for our baby?
Haben Sie ein Kinderbett für unser Baby?
***hab**-en zee yn **kind**-er-bet für oons-er **bayb**-ee*

Is there a paddling pool?
Haben Sie ein Planschbecken?
***hab**-en zee yn **plansh**-bek-en*

Is there a swimming pool?
Haben Sie ein Schwimmbecken?
***hab**-en zee yn **shvim**-bek-en*

Is there a swing park?
Haben Sie Schaukeln?
***hab**-en zee **showk**-eln*

It will not happen again
Es wird nicht wieder vorkommen
*es virt **neekht** veed-er **foar**-kom-en*

My daughter is 7 years old
Meine Tochter ist sieben Jahre alt.
*myn-e **tokht**-er ist zeeb-en **yar**-e alt*

Childcare

My son is 10 years old
Mein Sohn ist zehn Jahre alt.
*myn **zoan** ist tsayn **yar**-e alt*

She goes to bed at nine o'clock
Sie geht um neun Uhr ins Bett
*zee gayt oom **noyn** oor ins **bet***

We will be back in two hours
Wir sind in zwei Stunden zurück
*veer zind in **tsvy shtoond**-en tsoo-**rûk***

Where can I buy some disposable nappies?
Wo kann ich Windelhöschen kaufen?
***voa** kan eekh **vind**-el-hoes-khen **kowf**-en*

Where can I change the baby?
Wo kann ich das Baby wickeln?
***voa** kan eekh das **bayb**-ee vik-eln*

Where can I feed/breastfeed my baby?
Wo kann ich mein Baby füttern/stillen?
***voa** kan eekh myn **bayb**-ee **fût**-ern/**shtil**-en*

GETTING AROUND

Asking for directions

Where is — the art gallery?
Wo ist — die Kunstgalerie?
voa ist — dee koonst-gal-er-ee

— the post office?
— das Postamt?
— das post-amt

— the Tourist Information Service?
— die Tourist Information?
— dee too-reest in-form-a-tsee-oan

Can you show me on the map?
Können Sie mir das auf der Karte zeigen?
koen-en zee meer das owf der kart-e tsyg-en

Can you tell me the way to the bus station?
Können Sie mir den Weg zum Bahnhof sagen?
koen-en zee meer den vayg tsoom ban-hoaf zag-en

Can you walk there?
Kann man dorthin zu Fuß gehen?
kan man dort-hin tsoo foos gay-en

I am looking for the Tourist Information Office
Ich suche die Tourist Information
eekh zookh-e dee too-reest in-form-a-tsee-oan

Where are the toilets?
Wo sind die Toiletten?
voa zint dee toy-let-en

Asking for directions

I am lost
Ich habe mich verlaufen
*eekh **hab**-e meekh fer-**lowf**-en*

I am lost. How do I get to the Krone Hotel?
Ich habe mich verlaufen. Wie finde ich das Hotel Krone?
*eekh **hab**-e meekh fer-**lowf**-en vee find-e eekh das hoa-**tel kroan**-e*

I am trying to get to the market
Ich versuche, zum Markt zu gehen
*eekh fer-**zookh**-e tsoom **markt** tsoo **gay**-en*

I want to go to the theatre
Ich möchte ins Theater gehen
*eekh **moekht**-e ins tay-a-ter **gay**-en*

Is it far?
Ist es weit?
*ist es **vyt***

Is there a bus that goes there?
Gibt es einen Bus, der dorthin fährt?
***gipt** es yn-en **boos** der **dort**-hin fert*

Is there a train that goes there?
Gibt es einen Zug, der dorthin fährt?
***gipt** es yn-en **tsoog** der **dort**-hin fert*

Is this the right way to the supermarket?
Ist das der richtige Weg zum Supermarkt?
*ist **das** der **reekht**-ig-e **vayg** tsoom **soop**-er-markt*

We are looking for a restaurant
Wir suchen ein Restaurant
*veer **zookh**-en yn rest-oa-**rong***

Asking for directions

Where do I get a bus for the city centre?
Wo finde ich einen Bus zur Innenstadt?
voa find-e eekh yn-en boos tsoor in-en-shtat

By road

Do I turn here for Bad Windsheim?
Muß ich nach Bad Windsheim hier abbiegen?
moos eekh nakh bat vints-hym heer ap-beeg-en

How far is it to Dresden?
Wie weit ist es nach Dresden?
vee vyt ist es nakh drays-den

How long will it take to get there?
Wie lange dauert es, bis man dorthin kommt?
vee lang-e dow-ert es bis man dort-hin komt

Is there a filling station near here?
Gibt es hier in der Nähe eine Tankstelle?
gipt es heer in der ne-e yn-e tank-shtel-e

I am looking for the next exit
Ich suche die nächste Ausfahrt
eekh zookh-e dee nekst-e ows-fart

Where does this road go to?
Wohin führt diese Straße?
voa-heen fûrt deez-e shtras-e

How do I get onto the motorway?
Wie komme ich auf die Autobahn?
vee kom-e eekh owf dee owt-o-ban

Directions

Which is the best route to Frankfurt?
Wie komme ich am besten nach Frankfurt?
vee kom-e eekh am best-en nakh frank-foort

Which road do I take to Aachen?
Welche Straße muß ich nach Aachen nehmen?
velkh-e shtras-e moos eekh nakh akh-en naym-en

Which is the fastest route?
Was ist die schnellste Route?
vas ist dee shnelst-e root-e

Will we arrive in time for dinner?
Werden wir rechtzeitig zum Abendessen ankommen?
vayrd-en veer rekht-tsyt-eekh tsoom ab-end-es-en an-kom-en

Directions

You go — as far as...
Sie fahren — bis...
zee far-en —bis...

> **— left**
> — nach links
> *—nakh links*

> **— right**
> — nach rechts
> *—nakh rekhts*

> **— towards...**
> — auf... zu
> *—owf... tsoo*

Directions

It is — at the intersection
Es ist — an der Kreuzung
*es ist — an der **kroyts**-oong*

— under the bridge
— unter der Brücke
*— oont-er der **brûk**-e*

— after the traffic lights
— nach der Ampel
*— nakh der **amp**-el*

— around the corner
— um die Ecke
*— oom dee **ek**-e*

— next to the cinema
— neben dem Kino
*— nayb-en dem **keen**-o*

— on the next floor
— auf dem nächsten Stockwerk
*— owf dem **nekst**-en **shtok**-verk*

— opposite the railway station
— gegenüber der Eisenbahn
*— gayg-en-**ûb**-er der **yz**-en-ban*

— over there
— da drüben
*— da **drûb**-en*

Cross the street
überqueren Sie die Straße
*ûb-er-**kvayr**-en zee dee **shtras**-e*

Directions

Turn left
Biegen Sie links ab
beeg-en zee links ap

Turn right
Biegen Sie rechts ab
beeg-en zee rekhts ap

Follow the signs for...
Folgen Sie den Zeichen nach...
folg-en zee den tsykh-en nakh...

— the motorway
— die Autobahn
— dee owt-o-ban

— the next junction
— die nächste Abzweigung
— dee nekst-e ap-tsvyg-oong

— the square
— der Platz
— der plats

Keep going straight ahead
Fahren Sie gerade aus
far-en zee ge-rad-e ows

Take the first road on the right
Biegen Sie bei der nächsten Straße rechts ab
beeg-en zee by der nekst-en shtras-e rekhts ap

You have to go back
Sie müssen zurückfahren
zee mûs-en tsoo-rûk-far-en

Directions

Take the road for Bamberg
Nehmen Sie die Straße nach Bamberg
naym-en zee dee stras-e nakh bam-berg

Take the second road on the left
Biegen Sie bei der zweiten Straße links ab
beeg-en zee by der tsvyt-en stras-e links ap

You have to pay the toll
Sie müssen eine Gebühr zahlen
zee mûs-en yn-e ge-bûr tsal-en

Hiring a car

Can I hire a car?
Kann ich einen Wagen mieten?
kan eekh yn-en vag-en meet-en

Can I hire a car with an automatic gearbox?
Kann ich einen Wagen mit Automatikschaltung mieten?
kan eekh yn-en vag-en mit owt-o-mat-eek-shalt-oong meet-en

I want to hire a car
Ich möchte einen Wagen mieten
eekh moekht-e yn-en vag-en meet-en

I need it for 2 weeks.
Ich brauche ihn für zwei Wochen.
eekh browkh-e een fûr tsvy vokh-en

We will both be driving
Wir werden beide fahren
veer vayrd-en byd-e far-en

Hiring a car

Do you have — a large car?
 Haben Sie — einen großen Wagen?
 hab-en zee —yn-en gros-en vag-en

                    — a smaller car?
                    — einen kleineren Wagen?
                    —eyn-en klyn-er-en vag-en

                    — an automatic?
                    — einen Wagen mit Automatikschaltung?
                    —yn-en vag-en mit owt-oa-mat-ik-shalt-oong

                    — an estate car?
                    — einen Kombiwagen?
                    —yn-en kom-bee-vag-en

I would like to leave the car at the airport
Ich möchte den Wagen am Flughafen stehen lassen
eekh moekht-e den vag-en am floog-haf-en shtay-en las-en

I want to leave a car at the airport
Ich möchte den Wagen am Flughafen lassen
eekh moekht-e den vag-en am floog-haf-en las-en

Is there a charge per kilometre?
Gibt es eine Gebühr pro Kilometer?
gipt es yn-e ge-bûr pro keel-o-mayt-er

Must I return the car here?
Muß ich den Wagen hierher zurückbringen?
moos eekh den vag-en heer-hayr tsu-rûk-bring-en

Please explain the documents
Bitte erklären Sie mir die Unterlagen
bit-e er-kler-en zee meer dee oont-er-lag-en

Hiring a car

How much is it per kilometre?
Wieviel kostet es pro Kilometer?
vee-feel kost-et es pro keel-o-mayt-er

Can I pay for insurance?
Kann ich gegen Gebühr eine Versicherung abschließen?
kan eekh gayg-en ge-bûr yn-e fer-zeekh-er-oong ap-shlees-en

Do I have to pay a deposit?
Muß ich etwas anzahlen?
moos eekh et-vas an-tsal-en

I would like a spare set of keys
Ich hätte gerne Extraschlüssel
eekh het-e gern-e ex-tra-shlûs-el

How does the steering lock work?
Wie funktioniert das Lenkradschloß?
vee foonk-tsee-o-neert das lenk-rat-shlos

 Please show me how — to operate the lights
Zeigen Sie mir bitte, wie — die Scheinwerfer bedient werden
tsyg-en zee meer bit-e vee —dee shyn-verf-er be-deent vayrd-en

 — to operate the windscreen wipers.
 — die Scheibenwischer betätigt werden.
 — dee shyb-en-vish-er be-tet-eegt vayrd-en

Where is reverse gear?
Wo ist der Rückwärtsgang?
voa ist der rûk-verts-gang

Where is the tool kit?
Wo ist das Werkzeug?
voa ist das verk-tsoyg

By taxi

Please show us around the town
Zeigen Sie uns bitte die Stadt
tsyg-en zee oons bit-e dee shtat

Please take me to this address
Bringen Sie mich bitte zu dieser Adresse
bring-en zee meekh bit-e tsoo deez-er a-dress-e

Take me to the airport, please
Bringen Sie mich bitte zum Flughafen
bring-en zee meekh bit-e tsoom floog-haf-en

The bus station, please
Die Bushaltestelle, bitte
dee boos-halt-e-shtel-e bit-e

Turn left, please
Nach links, bitte
nakh links bit-e

Turn right, please
Nach rechts, bitte
nakh rekhts bit-e

Can you come back in one hour?
Können Sie in einer Stunde zurückkommen?
koen-en zee in yn-er shtoond-e tsoo-rûk-kom-en

Will you put the bags in the boot?
Könnten Sie das Gepäck bitte in den Kofferraum legen?
koent-en zee das ge-pek bit-e in den kof-er-rowm layg-en

By taxi

I am in a hurry
Ich bin in Eile
eekh bin in yl-e

Please hurry, I am late
Bitte beeilen Sie sich, ich habe bereits Verspätung
bit-e be-yl-en zee zeekh eekh hab-e be-ryts fer-shpet-oong

Please wait here for a few minutes
Bitte warten Sie hier ein paar Minuten
bit-e vart-en zee heer yn par mee-noot-en

Please, stop at the corner
An der Ecke bitte halten
an der ek-e bit-e halt-en

Please, wait here
Bitte warten Sie hier
bit-e vart-en zee heer

Wait for me please
Bitte warten Sie auf mich
bit-e vart-en zee owf meekh

How much is that, please?
Was macht das, bitte?
vas makht das bit-e

Keep the change
Der Rest ist für Sie
der rest ist fûr zee

By bus

Does this bus go to the castle?
Fährt dieser Bus zur Burg?
*fert deez-er **boos** tsoor **boorg***

How frequent is the service?
In welchen Abständen fährt der Bus?
*in **velkh**-em **ap**-stend-en **fert** der **boos***

How long does it take to get to the park?
Wie lange dauert es bis zum Park?
*vee **lang**-e **dow**-ert es bis tsoom **park***

Is there a bus into town?
Gibt es einen Bus in die Stadt?
*gipt es yn-en **boos** in dee **shtat***

What is the fare to the city centre?
Was kostet die Fahrt in die Innenstadt?
*vas **kost**-et dee **fart** in dee **in**-en-shtat*

When is the last bus?
Wann geht der letzte Bus?
*van **gayt** der **letst**-e **boos***

Where do I get the bus for the airport?
Wo kann ich den Bus zum Flughafen nehmen?
***voa** kan eekh den **boos** tsoom **floog**-haf-en **naym**-en*

Where should I change?
Wo muß ich umsteigen?
***voa** moos eekh **oom**-shtyg-en*

By bus

Which bus do I take for the football stadium?
Welcher Bus fährt zum Fußballstadium?
*velkh-er **boos** fert tsoom **foos**-bal-**stad**-ee-oom*

Will you tell me when to get off the bus?
Könnten Sie mir sagen, wann ich aussteigen muß?
koent**-en zee meer **zag**-en van eekh **ows**-shtyg-en **moos

By train

A return (ticket) to Hamburg, please
Eine Rückfahrkarte nach Hamburg, bitte
*yn-e **rûk**-far-kart-e nakh **ham**-boorg **bit**-e*

A return to Paris, first-class
Eine Rückfahrkarte erster Klasse nach Paris, bitte
*yn-e **rûk**-far-kart-e erst-er **klas**-e nakh pa-**rees** bit-e*

A single (one-way ticket) to Hannover, please
Eine Einzelfahrkarte (Rückfahrkarte) nach Hannover, bitte
*yn-e **yn**-tsel-far-kart-e (**rûk**-far-kart-e) nakh han-**oaf**-er **bit**-e*

Can I buy a return ticket?
Kann ich eine Rückfahrkarte kaufen?
***kan** eekh yn-e **rûk**-far-kart-e **kowf**-en*

I want to book a seat on the sleeper to Paris
Ich möchte einen Platz im Schlafwagen nach Paris buchen
*eekh **moekht**-e yn-en **plats** im **shlaf**-vag-en nakh pa-**rees** **bookh**-en*

By train

Second class. A window seat, please
Zweiter Klasse. Einen Fensterplatz, bitte
tsvyt-er klas-e yn-en fenst-er-plats bit-e

What are the times of the trains to Paris?
Was sind die Zeiten für die Züge nach Paris?
vas zint dee tsyt-en für dee tsûg-e nakh pa-rees

Where can I buy a ticket?
Wo kann ich eine Fahrkarte kaufen?
voa kan eekh yn-e far-kart-e kowf-en

A smoking compartment, first-class
Ein Raucherabteil erster Klasse
yn rowkh-er-ap-tyl erst-er klas-e

A non-smoking compartment, please
Ein Nichtraucherabteil bitte
yn neekht-rowkh-er-ap-tyl bit-e

When is the next train to Munich?
Wann geht der nächste Zug nach München?
van gayt der nekst-e tsoog nakh mûn-khen

When is the next train to Stuttgart?
Wann geht der nächste Zug nach Stuttgart?
van gayt der nekst-e tsoog nakh shtoot-gart

How long do I have before my next train leaves?
Wieviel Zeit habe ich bis zur Abfahrt meines nächsten Zuges?
vee-feel tsyt hab-e eekh bis tsoor ap-fart myn-es nekst-en tsoog-es

Do I have time to go shopping?
Habe ich noch Zeit zum Einkaufen?
hab-e eekh nokh tsyt tsoom yn-kowf-en

By train

Can I take my bicycle?
Kann ich mein Rad mitnehmen?
*kan eekh myn **rat** mit-naym-en*

What time does the train leave?
Wann fährt der Zug ab?
*van fert der **tsoog** ap*

What time is the last train?
Wann geht der letzte Zug?
*van gayt der **letst**-e tsoog*

Where do I have to change?
Wo muß ich umsteigen?
*voa moos eekh **oom**-shtyg-en*

I want to leave these bags in the left-luggage
Ich möchte diese Taschen bei der Gepäckverwahrung lassen
*eekh **moekht**-e deez-e **tash**-en by der ge-**pek**-fer-**var**-oong **las**-en*

Can I check in my bags?
Kann ich mein Gepäck aufgeben?
*kan eekh myn ge-**pek** owf-geb-en*

How much is it per bag?
Wieviel kostet es pro Gepäckstück?
*vee-**feel** kost-et es pro ge-**pek**-shtûk*

I shall pick them up this evening
Kann ich sie heute Abend abholen?
kan eekh zee hoyt-e ab-ent ap-hoal-en

Where do I pick up my bags?
Wo kann ich mein Gepäck abholen?
*voa kan eekh myn ge-**pek** ap-hoal-en*

By train

Is there — a buffet car (club car)?
Gibt es — eine Snackbar (einen Salonwagen?)
gipt es — yn-e snak-bar (yn-en za-loang-vag-en

> **— a dining car?**
> — einen Speisewagen?
> *— yn-en shpyz-e-vag-en*

Is there a restaurant on the train?
Hat der Zug einen Speisewagen?
hat der tsoog yn-en shpyz-e-vag-en

Where is the departure board (listing)?
Wo ist der Abfahrtsplan?
voa ist der ap-farts-plan

Which platform do I go to?
Zu welchem Bahnsteig muß ich gehen?
tsoo velkh-em ban-shtyg moos eekh gay-en

Is this the platform for Mannheim?
Ist das der richtige Bahnsteig für den Zug nach Mannheim?
ist das der reekht-ig-e ban-shtyg für den tsoog nakh man-hym

Is this a through train?
Ist das ein Direktzug?
ist das yn dee-rekt-tsoog

Is this the Bonn train?
Ist das der Zug nach Bonn?
ist das der tsoog nakh bon

Do we stop at Schwabach?
Halten wir in Schwabach?
halt-en veer in shvab-akh

By train

What time do we get to Hildesheim?
Wann kommen wir in Hildesheim an?
*van kom-en veer in **hild**-es-hym an*

Are we at Hof yet?
Sind wir schon in Hof?
*zint veer shoan in **hoaf***

Are we on time?
Wird der Zug rechtzeitig ankommen?
*virt der **tsoog rekh**-tsyt-eekh **an**-kom-en*

Can you help me with my bags?
Könnten Sie mir bitte mit meinem Gepäck helfen?
***koent**-en zee meer **bit**-e mit myn-em ge-**pek helf**-en*

I have lost my ticket
Ich habe meine Fahrkarte verloren
*eekh **hab**-e myn-e **far**-kart-e fer-**loar**-en*

My wife has my ticket
Meine Frau hat meine Fahrkarte
*myn-e **frow** hat myn-e **far**-kart-e*

Is this seat taken?
Ist dieser Platz besetzt?
*ist deez-er **plats** be-**zetst***

May I open the window?
Darf ich das Fenster öffnen?
***darf** eekh das **fenst**-er **oef**-nen*

This is a non-smoking compartment
Das ist ein Nichtraucherabteil
das** ist yn **neekht**-rowkh-er-ap-**tyl

By train

This is my seat
Das ist mein Platz
das ist myn plats

Where is the toilet?
Wo sind die Toiletten?
voa zint dee toy-let-en

Why have we stopped?
Warum haben wir angehalten?
va-room hab-en veer an-ge-halt-en

DRIVING

Traffic and weather conditions

Are there any hold-ups?
Gibt es Verkehrsstörungen?
gipt es fer-kayrs-stoer-oong-en

Is there a different way to the stadium?
Gibt es eine andere Route zum Stadium?
gipt es yn-e and-er-e root-e tsoom shtad-ee-oom

Is there a toll on this motorway?
Ist diese Autobahn gebührenpflichtig?
ist deez-e owt-o-ban ge-bûr-en-pfleekht-eekh

What is causing this traffic jam?
Wodurch wird dieser Stau verursacht?
voa-doorkh virt deez-er shtow fer-oor-zakht

What is the speed limit?
Was ist die Höchstgeschwindigkeit?
vas ist dee hoekst-ge-shvind-eekh-kyt

When is the rush hour?
Wann sind die Stoßzeiten?
van zint dee shtoas-tsyt-en

Is the traffic heavy?
Gibt es viel Verkehr
gipt es feel fer-kayr

Is the traffic one-way?
Ist das eine Einbahnstraße?
ist das yn-e yn-ban-shtras-e

When will the road be clear?
Wann ist die Straße wieder frei?
van ist dee stras-e veed-er fry

Do I need snow chains?
Brauche ich Schneeketten?
browkh-e eekh shnay-ket-en

Is the pass open?
Ist der Paß geöffnet?
ist der pas ge-oef-net

Is the road to Saarbrücken snowed up?
Ist die Strecke nach Saarbrücken verschneit?
ist dee shtrek-e nakh zar-brûk-en fer-shnyt

Parking

Where is there a car park?
Wo gibt es hier einen Parkplatz?
voa gipt es heer yn-en park-plats

Can I park here?
Kann ich hier parken?
kan eekh heer park-en

Do I need a parking disc?
Brauche ich hier eine Parkscheibe?
browkh-e eekh heer yn-e park-shyb-e

Where can I get a parking disc?
Wo kann ich eine Parkscheibe bekommen?
voa kan eekh yn-e park-shyb-e be-kom-en

Parking

How long can I stay here?
Wie lange kann ich hier bleiben?
*vee **lang**-e kan eekh heer **blyb**-en*

Is it safe to park here?
Kann man hier unbesorgt parken?
*kan man heer **oon**-be-zorgt **park**-en*

What time does the car park/multi-storey car park close?
Wann schließt der Parkplatz/Parkhaus?
*van shleest der **park**-plats/das **park**-hows*

Where do I pay?
Wo kann ich zahlen?
*voa kan eekh **tsal**-en*

Do I need coins for the meter?
Brauche ich Münzen für die Parkuhr?
*browkh-e eekh **mûnts**-en fûr dee **park**-oor*

Do I need parking lights?
Brauche ich eine Parkleuchte?
*browkh-e eekh yn-e **park**-loykht-e*

At the service station

Do you take credit cards?
Kann ich mit Kreditkarte zahlen?
*kan eekh mit kray-**deet**-kart-e **tsal**-en*

Fill the tank please
Voll bitte
fol bit-e

At the service station

25 litres of — unleaded petrol
25 Liter — bleifreies Benzin
fûnf-oont-tsvant-seekh lee-ter — bly-fry-es ben-tseen

— 3 star
— Normalbenzin
—nor-mal-ben-tseen

— 4 star
— Super
—soop-er

— diesel
— Diesel
—deez-el

Can you clean the windscreen?
Können Sie die Windschutzscheibe putzen?
koen-en zee dee vint-shoots-shyb-e poots-en

Check — the oil
Prüfen Sie bitte — den Ölstand
prûf-en zee bit-e —den oel-shtant

— the water
— das Wasser
—das vas-er

Check the tyre pressure please
Bitte prüfen Sie den Reifendruck
bit-e prûf-en zee den ryf-en-drook

The pressure should be 2.3 at the front and 2.5 at the rear
Der Druck sollte vorne 2,3 und hinten 2,5 sein
der drook solt-e forn-e tsvy-dry oont hint-en tsvy-fûnf zyn

At the service station

I need some distilled water
Ich brauche destilliertes Wasser
*eekh **browkh**-e de-steel-eert-es **vas**-er*

Breakdowns and repairs

Is there a telephone nearby?
Gibt es hier in der Nähe ein Telefon?
***gipt** es heer in der **ne**-e yn **tay**-lay-foan*

Can you send a recovery truck?
Können Sie einen Abschleppdienst senden?
***koen**-en zee yn-en **ap**-shlep-deenst **zen**-den*

Can you take me to the nearest garage?
Können Sie mich zur nächsten Werkstatt bringen?
***koen**-en zee meekh tsoor **nekst**-en **verk**-shtat **bring**-en*

I have run out of petrol.
Ich habe kein Benzin mehr.
*eekh **hab**-e kyn ben-**tseen** mayr*

Can you give me a can of petrol, please?
Könnten Sie mir bitte einen Kanister Benzin geben?
***koent**-en zee meer **bit**-e yn-en kan-**eest**-er ben-**tseen** gayb-en*

Can you give me — a push?
Könnten Sie mich bitte — anschieben?
***koent**-en zee meekh **bit**-e — **an**-sheeb-en*

— a tow?
— abschleppen?
***— ap**-shlep-en*

Breakdowns and repairs

Is there a mechanic here?
Ist ein Mechaniker da?
*ist yn me-**khan**-ee-ker da*

Do you have an emergency fan belt?
Haben Sie einen Reservekeilriemen?
***hab**-en zee yn-en re-**zerv**-e-kyl-reem-en*

Do you have jump leads?
Haben Sie ein Starthilfekabel?
***hab**-en zee yn **shtart**-hilf-e-kab-el*

Can you find out what the trouble is?
Können Sie feststellen, was das Problem ist?
***koen**-en zee **fest**-shtel-en vas das **prob**-laym ist*

There is something wrong
Etwas funktioniert nicht
*et-vas **foonk**-tsee-oa-**neert** neekht*

There is something wrong with the car
Mit dem Auto stimmt etwas nicht
*mit dem **owt**-oa **shtimt** et-vas **neekht***

Will it take long to repair it?
Würde eine Reparatur lang dauern?
*vûrd-e yn-e re-pa-ra-**toor** lang **dow**-ern*

Is it serious?
Ist es etwas Größeres?
***ist** es et-vas **groes**-er-es*

Can you repair it for the time being?
Können Sie es übergangsweise reparieren?
***koen**-en zee es **ûb**-er-gangz-vyz-e re-pa-**reer**-en*

Breakdowns and repairs

Can you replace the windscreen wiper blades?
Können Sie die Scheibenwischergummis ersetzen?
koen-en zee dee shyb-en-vish-er-goom-eez er-zets-en

Can you repair a flat tyre?
Können Sie einen platten Reifen reparieren?
koen-en zee yn-en plat-en ryf-en re-pa-reer-en

Do you have the spare parts?
Haben Sie Ersatzteile?
hab-en zee er-zats-tyl-e

I have a flat tyre
Ich habe einen platten Reifen
eekh hab-e yn-en plat-en ryf-en

I have locked myself out of the car
Ich habe mich aus dem Wagen ausgesperrt
eekh hab-e meekh ows dem vag-en ows-ge-spert

I have locked the ignition key inside the car
Ich habe den Zündschlüssel im Auto eingeschlossen
eekh hab-e den tsûnt-shlûs-el im owt-oa yn-ge-shlos-en

I need a new fan belt
Ich brauche einen neuen Keilriemen
eekh browkh-e yn-en noy-en kyl-reem-en

I think there is a bad connection
Ich glaube, da ist ein Wackelkontakt
eekh glowb-e da ist yn vak-el-kon-takt

My car has been towed away
Mein Wagen wurde abgeschleppt
myn vag-en voord-e ap-ge-shlept

Breakdowns and repairs

My car has broken down
Mein Auto hatte eine Panne
*myn **owt**-o hat-e yn-e **pan**-e*

My car will not start
Mein Wagen springt nicht an
*myn **vag**-en **shpring**t **neekht** an*

My windscreen has cracked
Meine Windschutzscheibe ist gesprungen
*myn-e **vint**-shuts-shyb-e ist ge-**shproong**-en*

The air-conditioning does not work
Die Klimaanlage funktioniert nicht
*dee **klee**-ma-an-lag-e **foonk**-tsee-oa-neert neekht*

The battery is flat
Die Batterie ist leer
*de bat-e-**ree** ist **layr***

The engine — has broken down
  Der Motor — ist kaputt
*der **moa**-toar —ist ka-**poot***

**   — is overheating**
        — ist überhitzt
*   —ist **ûb**-er-**hitst***

The exhaust pipe has fallen off
Der Auspuff ist abgefallen
*der **ows**-poof ist **ap**-ge-fal-en*

There is a leak in the radiator
Die Kühlung ist undicht
*dee **kûl**-oong ist **oon**-deekht*

Accidents and the Police

Accidents and the Police

There has been an accident
Ein Unfall ist passiert
yn oon-fal ist pa-seert

We must call — an ambulance
  Wir müssen — den Notarzt rufen
  veer mûs-en — den noat-artst roof-en

             — the police
             — die Polizei rufen
             — dee pol-ee-tsy roof-en

What is your name and address?
Was sind Ihr Name und Ihre Adresse?
vas zint eer nam-e oont eer-e a-dress-e

You must not move
Sie dürfen sich nicht bewegen
zee dûrf-en zeekh neekht be-vayg-en

I could not stop in time
Ich konnte nicht rechtzeitig zum Stehen kommen
eekh kont-e neekht rekht-tsyt-eekh tsoom shtay-en kom-en

I did not know about the speed limit
Ich wußte nichts von der Geschwindigkeitsbegrenzung
eekh voost-e neekhts fon der ge-shvind-eekh-kyts-be-grents-oong

I did not see the bicycle
Ich habe das Fahrrad nicht gesehen
eekh hab-e das far-rat neekht ge-zay-en

Accidents and the Police

He did not stop
Er hat nicht angehalten
*er hat neekht **an**-ge-halt-en*

He is a witness
Er ist Zeuge
*er ist **tsoyg**-e*

He overtook on a bend
Er überholte in einer Kurve
*er ûb-er-**holt**-e in yn-er **koorv**-e*

He ran into the back of my car
Er fuhr auf meinen Wagen auf
*er **foor** owf myn-en **vag**-en owf*

He stopped suddenly
Er bremste plötzlich
*er **bremst**-e **ploets**-leekh*

He was moving too fast
Er ist zu schnell gefahren
*er ist tsoo **shnel** ge-**far**-en*

I did not see the sign
Ich habe das Zeichen nicht gesehen
*eekh **hab**-e das **tsykh**-en neekht ge-**zay**-en*

Here are my insurance documents
Hier sind meine Versicherungsunterlagen
***heer** zint myn-e fer-**seekh**-er-oongs-**oont**-er-lag-en*

Here is my driving licence
Da ist mein Führerschein
*da ist myn **fûr**-er-shyn*

Accidents and the Police

I cannot find my driving licence
Ich kann meinen Führerschein nicht finden
eekh **kan** *myn-en* **für-**er-shyn neekht **find-**en

Do you want my credit card?
Brauchen Sie meine Kreditkarte?
browkh-en zee myn-e kray-**deet-**kart-e

Do you want my passport?
Brauchen Sie meinen Paß?
browkh-en zee myn-en **pas**

I am very sorry. I am a visitor
Es tut mir sehr leid. Ich bin nur zu Besuch hier
es **toot** *meer zayr* **lyt** *eekh bin* **noor** *tsoo be-***zookh** *heer*

I did not understand the sign
Ich habe das Zeichen nicht verstanden
eekh **hab-**e das **tsykh-**en neekht fer-**shtand-**en

How much is the fine?
Wie hoch ist die Geldbuße?
vee **hoakh** *ist dee* **gelt-**boos-e

I have not got enough money. Can I pay at the police station?
Ich habe nicht genug Geld. Kann ich bei der Polizeiwache zahlen?
eekh **hab-**e neekht ge-noog **gelt.** **kan** eekh by der pol-ee-tsy-vakh-e **tsal-**en

I was only driving at 50 km/h
Ich bin nur 50 km/h gefahren
eekh **bin** *noor* **fünf-**tseekh kee-loa-**mayt-**er pro **shtoond-**e ge-**far-**en

Accidents and the Police

I have not had anything to drink
Ich habe nichts getrunken
*eekh **hab**-e neekhts ge-**troonk**-en*

I was overtaking
Ich habe überholt
*eekh **hab**-e ûb-er-**hoalt***

I was parking
Ich habe geparkt
*eekh **hab**-e ge-**parkt***

That car was too close
Dieser Wagen hielt nicht genügend Abstand
*deez-er **vag**-en heelt **neekht** ge-**nûg**-end **ap**-stand*

The brakes failed
Die Bremsen versagten
*dee **bremz**-en fer-**zagt**-en*

The car number was...
Das Nummernschild war...
*das **noom**-ern-shilt var... —*

The car skidded
Der Wagen schleuderte
*der **vag**-en **shloyd**-ert-e*

The car swerved
Der Wagen scherte aus
*der **vag**-en **shayrt**-e **ows***

The car turned right without signalling
Der Wagen bog rechts ab, ohne zu blinken.
*der **vag**-en boag **rekhts** ap oan-e tsoo **blink**-en*

Accidents and the Police

The road was icy
Die Straße war vereist
dee stras-e var fer-yst

The tyre burst
Der Reifen platzte
der ryf-en platst-e

Car parts

accelerator
Gaspedal
gas-pay-dal

aerial
Antenne
an-ten-e

air filter
Luftfilter
looft-filt-er

alternator
Drehstromgenerator
dray-stroam-gay-nay-ra-tor

antifreeze
Frostschutzmittel
frost-shoots-mit-el

automatic gearbox
Automatikschaltung
owt-oa-ma-teek-shalt-oong

axle
Achse
aks-e

battery
Batterie
bat-e-ree

bonnet
Kühlerhaube
kûl-er-howb-e

boot
Kofferraum
kof-er-rowm

brake fluid
Bremsenflüssigkeit
bremz-en-flûs-eekh-kyt

brake light
Bremsleuchte
bremz-loykht-e

Car parts

brakes
Bremsen
bremz-en

bulb
Glühbirne
glû-birn-e

bumper
Stoßstange
shtoas-shtang-e

car-phone
Autotelefon
owt-oa-tay-lay-foan

carburettor
Vergaser
fer-gas-er

child seat
Kindersitz
kind-er-zits

choke
Choke
tshoak

clutch
Kupplung
koop-loong

cooling system
Kühlung
kûl-oong

cylinder
Zylinder
tsû-lind-er

disc brake
Scheibenbremse
shyb-en-bremz-e

distributor
Verteiler
fer-tyl-er

door
Tür
tûr

dynamo
Lichtmaschine
leekht-ma-sheen-e

electrical system
Stromanlage
shtroam-an-lag-e

engine
Motor
moa-toar

exhaust system
Auspuffanlage
ows-poof-an-lag-e

fan belt
Keilriemen
kyl-reem-en

Car parts

foot pump
Fußpumpe
foos-poomp-e

fuel gauge
Benzinanzeige
ben-tseen-an-tsyg-e

fuel pump
Benzinpumpe
ben-tseen-poomp-e

fuse
Sicherung
zeekh-er-oong

gear box
Gangschaltung
gang-shalt-oong

gear lever
Hebel der Gangschaltung
hayb-el der gang-shalt-oong

generator
Generator
gay-nay-ra-tor

hammer
Hammer
ham-er

hand brake
Handbremse
hant-bremz-e

hazard lights
Warnblinkanlage
varn-blink-an-lag-e

headlights
Scheinwerfer
shyn-verf-er

heating system
Heizung
hyts-oong

hood
Haube
howb-e

horn
Hupe
hoop-e

hose
Schlauch
shlowkh

ignition key
Zündungsschlüssel
tsûnd-oongs-shlûs-el

ignition
Zündung
tsûnd-oong

indicator
Blinker
blink-er

Car parts

jack
Wagenheber
vag-en-hayb-er

lights
Leuchten
loykht-en

lock
Schloß
shlos

oil filter
Ölfilter
oel-filt-er

oil
Öl
oel

oil pressure
Ölstand
oel-shtant

petrol
Benzin
ben-tseen

points
Anschlüsse
an-shlûs-e

pump
Pumpe
poomp-e

radiator
Kühlung
kûl-oong

rear-view mirror
Rückscheibe
rûk-shyb-e

reflectors
Reflektoren
reflek-toar-en

reversing light
Rückfahrscheinwerfer
rûk-far-shyn-verf-er

roof-rack
Dachgepäckträger
dakh-ge-pek-treg-er

screwdriver
Schraubenzieher
shrowb-en-tsee-er

seat belt
Sicherheitsgurt
zeekh-er-hyts-goort

seat
Platz
plats

shock absorber
Stoßdämpfer
shtoas-dempf-er

Car parts

silencer
Schalldämpfer
shal-dempf-er

socket set
Steckschlüsselset
shtek-shlûs-el-set

spanner
Schraubenschlüssel
shrowb-en-shlûs-el

spare part
Ersatzteil
er-zats-tyl

spark plug
Zündkerze
tsûnd-kerts-e

speedometer
Geschwindigkeitsmesser
ge-shvind-eekh-kyts-mes-er

starter motor
Anlasser
an-las-er

steering
Lenkung
lenk-oong

steering wheel
Lenkrad
lenk-rat

sun roof
Schiebedach
sheeb-e-dakh

suspension
Federung
fay-der-oong

tools
Werkzeug
verk-tsoyg

towbar
Abschleppstange
ap-shlep-shtang-e

transmission
Getriebe
ge-treeb-e

tyre pressure
Reifendruck
ryf-en-drook

tyre
Reifen
ryf-en

warning light
Warnleuchte
varn-loykht-e

water
Wasser
vas-er

Road signs

wheel
Rad
rat

windshield
Frontscheibe
front-shyb-e

windscreen
Windschutzscheibe
vint-shoots shyb-e

wipers
Scheibenwischer
shyb-en-vish-er

Road signs

bitte rechts fahren
bit-e rekhts far-en
keep to the right

Durchfahrt verboten
doorkh-fart fer-boat-en
no thoroughfare

kein Eingang
kyn yn-gang
no entry

private Zufahrt
pree-vat-e tsoo-fart
private road

Parken nur für Anwohner
park-en noor für an-voan-er
parking for residents only

Umleitung
oom-lyt—oong
diversion

Eating Out

Reservations

Should we reserve a table?
Sollten wir einen Tisch bestellen?
sollt-en veer yn-en tish be-shtel-en

Can I book a table for four at 8 o'clock?
Kann ich für acht Uhr einen Tisch für vier Personen buchen?
kan eekh für akht oor yn-en tish für feer per-zoan-en bookh-en

Can we have a table for four?
Könnten wir bitte einen Tisch für vier Personen haben?
koent-en veer bit-e yn-en tish für feer per-zoan-en hab-en

I am a vegetarian
Ich bin Vegetarier
eekh bin veg-e-ta-reer-er

We would like a table — by the window
Wir hätten gerne einen Tisch — am Fenster
verr het-en gern-e yn-en tish — am fenst-er

— on the terrace
— auf der Terrasse
— owf der te-ras-e

Useful questions

Do you have a local speciality?
Haben Sie eine Spezialität des Ortes?
hab-en zee yn-e shpe-tsee-a-lee-tet des ort-es

Useful questions

Do you have a set menu?
Haben Sie ein Menü
hab-en zee yn me-nû

Do you have yoghurt?
Haben sie Joghurt?
hab-en zee yoa-goort

What do you recommend?
Was können Sie empfehlen?
vas koen-en zee emp-fayl-en

What is the dish of the day?
Was ist das Gericht des Tages?
vas ist das ge-reekht des tag-es

What is the soup of the day?
Was ist die Tagessuppe?
vas ist dee tag-es-zoop-e

What is this called?
Wie heißt das?
vee hyst das

What is this dish like?
Wie schmeckt dieses Gericht?
vee shmekt deez-es ge-reekht

Which local wine do you recommend?
Welchen hiesigen Wein empfehlen Sie?
velkh-en heez-ig-en vyn emp-fayl-en zee

How do I eat this?
Wie esse ich das?
vee es-e eekh das

Useful questions

Are vegetables included?
Ist das Gemüse inbegriffen?
*ist das ge-**mûz**-e **in**-be-grif-en*

Is the local wine good?
Ist der hiesige Wein gut?
*ist der **heez**-ig-e vyn goot*

Is this cheese very strong?
Ist das ein sehr kräftiger Käse?
*ist das yn zayr **kreft**-eg-er **kez**-e*

Is this good?
Ist das gut?
*ist das **goot***

Ordering your meal

I will take the set menu
Ich nehme das Menü
*eekh **naym**-e das me-**nû***

The menu, please
Die Karte, bitte
*dee **kart**-e **bit**-e*

I will take that
Ich nehme das
*eekh **naym**-e das*

That is for me
Das ist für mich
das** ist **fûr meekh

Ordering your meal

Can we start with soup?
Können wir mit einer Suppe anfangen?
koen-en veer mit yn-er zoop-e an-fang-en

I will have salad
Ich hätte gerne einen Salat
eekh het-e gern-e yn-en za-lat

Could we have some butter?
Könnten wir etwas Butter haben?
koent-en veer et-vas boot-er hab-en

Can we have some bread?
Können wir Brot haben?
koen-en veer broat hab-en

I like my steak — very rare
Ich bevorzuge mein Steak — sehr wenig durchgebraten
*eekh be-foar-tsoog-e myn stayk —zayr vayn-eekh
doorkh-ge-brat-en*

— **medium rare**
— mittel
—*mit-el*

— **rare**
— nicht sehr stark
durchgebraten
—*neekht zayr shtark
doorkh-ge-brat-en*

— **well done**
— durchgebraten
—*doorkh-ge-brat-en*

Ordering your meal

Could we have some more bread, please?
Könnten wir bitte noch etwas Brot haben?
koent-en veer bit-e nokh et-was broat hab-en

Can I see the menu again, please?
Kann ich bitte die Karte noch einmal sehen?
kan eekh bit-e dee kart-e nokh yn-mal zay-en

Ordering drinks

The wine list, please
Die Weinkarte bitte
dee vyn-kart-e bit-e

We will take the Riesling
Wir nehmen den Riesling
veer naym-en den reez-ling

A bottle of house red wine, please
Eine Flasche roten Hauswein, bitte
yn-e flash-e roat-en hows-vyn bit-e

A glass of dry white wine, please
Ein Glas trockenen Weißwein, bitte
yn glas trok-en-en vys-vyn bit-e

Another bottle of red wine, please
Noch eine Flasche Rotwein, bitte
nokh yn-e flash-e roat-vyn bit-e

Another glass, please
Noch ein Glas, bitte
nokh yn glas bit-e

Paying the bill

Black coffee, please
Schwarzen Kaffee, bitte
shvarts-en ka-fay bit-e

Coffee with milk, please
Kaffee mit Milch, bitte
ka-fay mit milkh bit-e

Some plain water, please
Könnten wir bitte etwas Leitungswasser haben?
koent-en veer bit-e et-was lyt-oongs-vas-er hab-en

Can we have some mineral water?
Können wir Mineralwasser haben?
koen-en veer min-er-al-vas-er hab-en

Two beers, please
Zwei Bier, bitte
tsvy beer bit-e

Paying the bill

Can we have the bill, please?
Könnten wir bitte die Rechnung haben?
koent-en veer bit-e dee rekh-noong hab-en

Can I have an itemized bill?
Könnte ich bitte eine spezifizierte Rechnung haben?
koent-e eekh bit-e yn-e shpets-ee-fee-tseert-e rekh-noong hab-en

Do you accept traveller's cheques?
Nehmen Sie Reiseschecks?
naym-en zee ryz-e-sheks

Paying the bill

Is service included?
Ist die Bedienung im Preis inbegriffen?
*ist dee be-**deen**-oong im **prys** **in**-be-grif-en*

Is tax included?
Ist die Steuer mitinbegriffen?
*ist dee **shtoy**-er mit-**in**-be-grif-en*

Is there any extra charge?
Gibt es zusätzliche Gebühren?
*gipt es **tsoo**-zets-leekh-e ge-**bûr**-en*

Can I have a receipt?
Könnte ich bitte eine Quittung haben?
***koent**-e eekh **bit**-e yn-e **kvit**-oong **hab**-en*

I would like to pay with my credit card
Ich möchte mit meiner Kreditkarte zahlen
*eekh **moekht**-e mit myn-er kray-**deet**-kart-e **tsal**-en*

I do not have enough currency
Ich habe nicht genug Landeswährung
*eekh hab-e **neekht** ge-noog **land**-es-ver-oong*

This is not correct
Das stimmt nicht
*das **shtimt** neekht*

This is not my bill
Das ist nicht meine Rechnung
*das ist neekht **myn**-e **rekh**-noong*

You have given me the wrong change
Sie haben mir falsch herausgegeben
*zee **hab**-en meer **falsh** hayr-**ows**-ge-gayb-en*

Complaints and compliments

This is cold
Das ist kalt
*das ist **kalt***

This is not what I ordered
Das ist nicht, was ich bestellt habe
*das ist **neekht** vas eekh be-**shtellt hab**-e*

Waiter! We have been waiting for a long time.
Herr Ober! Wir warten jetzt schon sehr lange.
*her **oab**-er veer **vart**-en yetst shoan zayr **lang**-e*

The meal was excellent
Das Essen war ausgezeichnet
*das es-en var **ows**-ge-tsykh-net*

This is excellent
Das ist ausgezeichnet
*das ist **ows**-ge-tsykh-net*

Can I have the recipe?
Könnte ich bitte das Rezept haben?
***koent**-e eekh bit-e das re-**tsept** hab-en*

Menu reader

Menu reader

Ananas
an-an-as
pineapple

Äpfel
ep-fel
apples

Apfelkompott
ap-fel-kom-pot
apple compote

Apfelkuchen
ap-fel-kookh-en
apple cake

Apfelpüree
ap-fel-pû-re
apple sauce

Aprikosen
ap-ree-koaz-en
apricots

Artischocken
ar-tee-shoak-en
artichoke

Aubergine
oa-ber-zheen-e
aubergine

Austern
owst-ern
oysters

Avocado
a-voa-ka-doa
avocado

Backhuhn/Brathuhn
bak-hoon/brat-hoon
baked/roasted chicken

Bananen
ba-na-nen
bananas

Barbe
barb-e
mullet

Basilikum
ba-zee-lee-koom
basil

Beefsteak
beef-stayk
beefsteak

Beignets
ben-ye
fritters

Menu reader

belegtes Brot
be-laygt-es broat
cold sandwich

Birne
birn-e
pear

Biskuitkuchen
bees-kveet-kookh-en
sponge cake

Blaue Zipfel
blow-e tsip-fel
sausages cooked with
vinegar and onions
(Frankonia)

Blumenkohl
bloom-en-koal
cauliflower

Blut- und Leberwurst
bloot oont layb-er-woorst
black pudding and liver
sausage (Frankonia)

Bohneneintopf
boan-en-yn-topf
bean stew

Bratapfel
brat-ap-fel
baked apple

Brathuhn/Backhuhn
brat-hoon/bak-hoon
fried/breaded chicken

Bratkartoffeln
brat-kar-tof-eln
roast potatoes

Brötchen
broet-khen
bread rolls

Brunnenkresse
broon-en-kres-e
watercress

Butter
boot-er
butter

Champignoncremesuppe
*shong-peen-yoang-kraym-
zoop-e*
cream of mushroom soup

**Champignons mit
Knoblauch**
*shong-peen-yoans mit
knoab-lowkh*
mushrooms with garlic

Champignons mit Soße
shong-peen-yoans mit zoas-e
mushrooms in sauce

Menu reader

Chicorée
shee-koa-ray
chicory

Cornichon
kor-nee-shoang
gherkin

Creme Caramel
kraym ka-ra-mel
caramel cream

Datteln
dat-eln
dates

Dessert
de-sert
pudding

dünne Pfannkuchen/Crêpes
dûn-e pfan-kookh-en/krep
thin pancakes

— mit Marmelade
— mit mar-me-lad-e
— with jam

— mit Schokolade
— mit shok-oa-lad-e
— with chocolate

Eier mit Schinken
y-er mit shink-en
eggs with ham

Eier mit Speck
y-er mit shpek
eggs with bacon

Eiernudeln
y-er-nood-eln
egg noodles

einfaches Kotelett
yn-fakh-es ko-te-let
plain cutlet

eingelegte Makrele
yn-ge-laygt-e mak-rayl-e
marinated mackerel

Eiskrem
ys-kraym
ice cream

Ente
ent-e
duck

Erbsen
erp-sen
peas

Erbsensuppe
erp-sen-soop-e
pea soup

Erdbeeren
ert-bayr-en
strawberries

Menu Reader

Erdbeeren mit Sahne
ert-bayr-en mit zan-e
strawberries with cream

Essig
es-eekh
vinegar

Estragon
es-tra-gon
tarragon

Fasan
fa-zan
pheasant

Filet
fee-lay
steak fillet

Fisch
fish
fish

Fleisch
flysh
meat

Fleisch vom Grill
flysh fom gril
grilled meats

Flußkrebs
floos-krayps
crayfish

Forelle blau
fo-rel-e blow
boiled trout

Forelle
fo-rel-e
trout

Forelle gebraten
fo-rel-e ge-brat-en
fried trout

französische Bohnen
fran-tsoe-zeesh-e boan-en
French beans

Gaisburger Marsch
gys-boorg-er marsh
stew with pasta and potatoes

Gans
gans
goose

gebratene Froschschenkel
ge-brat-en-e frosh-shenk-el
fried frog legs

gefüllter Hase
ge-fûl-ter haz-e
stuffed rabbit

gemischter Salat
ge-misht-er za-lat
mixed salad

Menu reader

Gemüse
ge-mûz-e
vegetables

Gemüsecremesuppe
ge-mûz-e-kraym-zoop-e
cream of vegetables soup

Granatäpfel
gra-nat-ep-fel
pomegranates

Grapefruit
grayp—froot
grapefruit

grüne Paprika
grûn-e pap-ree-ka
green pepper

grüner Pfeffer
grûn-er pfef-er
green pepper

Gurke
goork-e
cucumber

Gurkensalat
goork-en-za-lat
cucumber salad

Halve Hahn
halv-e han
cheese roll (Cologne)

Haxe (Lammshaxe)
haks-e (lams-hax-e)
leg (of lamb, etc)

Hechtfilet
hekht-fee-lay
hake fillet

Himbeeren
him-bayr-en
raspberries

Hühnerbrühe
hûn-er-brû-e
chicken broth

Hühnereintopf
hûn-er-yn-topf
chicken stew

Hühnersuppe
hûn-er-zoop-e
chicken soup

Hummer
hoom-er
lobster

Joghurt
yoa-goort
yoghurt

Kalbskotelett
kalps-ko-te-let
veal cutlet

Menu reader

Karotten
ka-rot-en
carrots

Kartoffelpüree
kar-tof-el-pû-ray
mashed potatoes

Kartoffelsalat
kar-to-fel-za-lat
potato salad

Käsekuchen
kez-e-kookh-en
cheese cake

Kerbel
ker-bel
chervil

Kirschen
kirsh-en
cherries

Knoblauch
knoab-lowkh
garlic

Knödel/Klöße
knoed-el/kloes-e
dumplings

Kohl/Weißkohl
koal/vys-koal
cabbage

Kopfsalat
kopf-za-lat
lettuce

Krapfen
krapf-en
doughnuts

Kuchen
kookh-en
cake

Kuchen
kookh-en
pie

Kürbis
kûr-bees
squash

Kutteln
koot-eln
tripe

Lamm am Spieß
lam am shpees
mutton on the spit

Lammkotelett
lam-kot-e-let
lamb cutlet

Lammshaxe
lams-hax-e
leg of lamb

Menu reader

Lauch
lowkh
leeks

Lauchsuppe
lowkh-zoope
leek soup

Leberkäse
layb-er-kez-e
processed meat (Bavaria)

Lorbeerblätter
loar-bayr-blet-er
bayleaf

Mais
ma-ees
sweet corn

Maissalat
ma-ees-za-lat
corn salad

Makrele
mak-rayl-e
mackerel

Mandelkuchen
mand-el-kookh-en
almond cake

Marillenknödel
ma-reel-en-knoed-el
potato dumplings filled
with apricots (Austria)

marinierter Fisch
ma-ree-neert-er fish
marinated fish

Markkürbis
mark-kûr-bis
marrow

Marmelade
mar-me-lad-e
jam

Maultaschen
mowl-tash-en
pasta filled with spinach
and chopped meat

Melone
me-loan-e
melon

Miesmuscheln
meez-moosh-eln
mussels

Milchreis
milkh-rys
rice pudding

Minze
mints-e
mint

Mousse au Chocolat
moos oa sho-koa-la
chocolate mousse

Menu reader

Muscheln
moosh-eln
clams

Niereneintopf
neer-en-yn-topf
stewed kidney

Nudeln
nood-eln
pasta

Obst mit Schlagsahne
obst mit shlag-zan-e
fruit with whipped cream

Obstsalat
obst-za-lat
fruit salad

Ochse am Spieß
oks-e am shpees
ox on the spit

Öl
oel
oil

Oliven
o-leev-en
olives

Orangen
o-ranzh-en
oranges

Palatschinken
pa-lat-shink-en
Austrian pancakes

Pasternake
past-er-nak-e
parsnip

Petersilie
payt-er-zeel-ee-e
parsley

Pfirsich
pfir-zeekh
peach

Pflaumen
pflowm-en
plums

Pilze/Champignons
pilts-e/shong-peen-yoans
mushrooms

Pommes frites
pom freet
French fries

Pumpernickel
poomp-er-nik-el
wholemeal bread

Radieschen
ra-dees-khen
radishes

Menu reader

Radieschen
ra-dees-khen
radishes

Räucherschinken
roykh-er-shink-en
cured ham

Reineclauden
ryn-e-kload
greengages

Rindereintopf
rind-er-yn-topf
beef stew

Rindsbrühe
rints-brû-e
beef broth

Rosenkohl
roaz-en-koal
Brussels sprouts

Rosenkohl
roaz-en-koal
Brussels sprouts

Rosmarin
roaz-mar-reen
rosemary

Rote Bete
roat-e bayt-e
beetroot

Rote Bete
roat-e bayt-e
beetroot

rote Paprika
roat-e pap-ree-ka
red pepper

Rote-Bohnen-Suppe
rot-e-boan-en-zoop-e
kidney-bean soup

Rühreier
rûr-y-er
scrambled eggs

russischer Salat
roos-eesh-er za-lat
Russian salad

Salat
za-lat
lettuce

Salat
za-lat
salad

Salbei
zal-by
sage

Sardinen
zar-deen-en
sardines

Menu reader

Sauerkraut
zow-er-krowt
pickled white cabbage

Saumagen
zow-mag-en
pork and processed meat

Scampi
skamp-ee
scampi

Schalotten
sha-lot-en
shallots

Schinkenbrot
shink-en-broat
ham sandwich

Schmorbraten
shmoar-brat-en
braised beef

Schnittbohnen
shnit-boan-en
broad beans

Schnittlauch
shnit-lowkh
chives

schwarze Johannisbeeren
shvarts-e joa-han-is-bayr-en
blackcurrants

Schweinebraten
shvyn-e-brat-en
pork roast

Schweinskotelett
shvyns-ko-te-let
pork cutlet

Soße mit grünem Pfeffer
zoas-e mit grün-em pfef-er
green pepper sauce

Spaghetti
shpa-get-ee
spaghetti

Spanferkel
shpan-ferk-el
suckling pig on the spit

Spargel
shparg-el
asparagus

Spiegeleier
shpeeg-el-y-er
eggs sunny side up

Spinat
spi-nat
spinach

Squash
skwosh
squash

Menu reader

Staudensellerie
shtowd-en-zel-er-ee
celery

Tafelspitz mit Kren
*taf-el-spits mit **krayn***
beef and horseradish

Thunfisch
toon-fish
tuna

Thymian
tûm-ee-an
thyme

Tintenfisch
tint-en-fish
cuttlefish

Tintenfisch
tint-en-fish
squid

Tomaten
*toa-**mat**-en*
tomatoes

Tomatensalat
*toa-**mat**-en-za-la*t
tomato salad

Tomatensoße
*toa-**mat**-en-zoas-e*
tomato sauce

Tomatensuppe
*toa-**mat**-en-**zoop**-e*
tomato soup

Trauben
trowb-en
grapes

Truthahn
troot-han
turkey

Vanillesauce
*fa-**neel**-e-zoas-e*
custard

vom Grill
*fom **gril***
grilled/barbecued

Wassermelone
vas-er-me-loan-e
watermelon

weichgekochtes Ei
***vykh**-ge-kokht-es y*
soft boiled egg

Weinsoße
***vyn**-zoas-e*
wine sauce

weiße Rüben
*vys-e **rûb**-en*
turnip

Drinks

Würstchen
vûrst-khen
sausage

Zitrone
tsee-troan-e
lemon

Zitronenbaiserkuchen
tsee-troan-en-be-zay-kookh-en
lemon meringue

Zucchini
tsoo-kee-nee
courgettes

Zuckererbsen
tsook-er-erps-en
sweet peas

Zunge
tsoong-e
tongue

Zwiebel
tsveeb-el
onion

Zwiebelsoße
tsveeb-el-zoas-e
onion sauce

Drinks

Apfelsaft
ap-fel-zaft
apple juice

Aprikosensaft
ap-ree-koz-en-zaft
apricot juice

Bananenmilch
ba-na-nen-milkh
banana milkshake

Bier
beer
beer

Bierflasche/Flaschenbier
beer-flash-e/flash-en-beer
bottled beer

Bowle
bow-le
punch

Calvados
kal-va-dos
apple brandy

Cappuccino
ka-poo-tshee-no
cappuccino

Drinks

Champagner/Sekt
*shong-**pan**-yer/zekt*
champagne

Cidre/Apfelwein
*seedr/**ap**-fel-vyn*
cider

Cola
koal-a
coke

Dosenbier
doaz-en-beer
canned beer

ein Glas Rotwein
*yn glas **roat**-vyna*
glass of red wine

ein Glas Weißwein
*yn glas **vys**-vyna*
glass of white wine

ein großes Bier
*yn gros-es **beer***
a large beer

ein Kännchen Kaffee
*yn **ken**-khen ka-fay*
small pot of coffee

ein Weinbrand
*yn **vyn**-brant*
a brandy

eine Tasse Kaffee
*yn-e **tas**-e ka-fay*
a cup of coffee

Eiskaffee
ys-ka-fayiced
coffee

entkoffeinierter Kaffee
ent-ko-fee-**neert**-er ka-fay
decaffeinated coffee

Grog
grog
tea with rum

Kaffee
ka-fay
coffee

Kaffee mit Milch
*ka-fay mit **milkh***
coffee with milk

Kaffee mit Milch
*ka-fay mit **milkh***
white coffee

Kamillentee
ka-meel-en-tay
camomile tea

Likör
*lee-**koer***
liqueur

Drinks

Limonade
lee-mo-nad-e
lemonade

löslicher Kaffee
loes-leekh-er ka-fay
instant coffee

Mineralwasser
mee-ner-al-vas-er
mineral water

Orangengetränk
o-ranzh-en-ge-trenk
orange drink

Orangensaft
o-ranzh-en-zaft
orange juice

Pfirsichsaft
pfir-zeekh-zaft
peach juice

Pharisäer
fa-reez-e-er
coffee with rum and cream

Roséwein
roa-zay-vyn
rosé wine

Rum
room
rum

Schnaps
shnaps
liquor

Sodawasser
zoad-a-vas-er
soda

Starkbier
shtark-beer
stout

Tee mit Milch
tay mit milkh
tea with milk

Tee mit Zitrone
tay mit tsee-troan-e
lemon tea

Tonic Wasser
ton-ik vas-er
tonic water

Traubensaft
trowb-en-zaft
grape juice

Wermut
vayr-moot
vermouth

Whisky
whisk-ee
whisky

OUT AND ABOUT

The weather

Is it going to get any warmer?
Wird es wärmer werden?
*virt es **verm**-er vayrd-en*

Is it going to stay like this?
Wird es so bleiben?
*virt es zo **blyb**-en*

Is there going to be a thunderstorm?
Wird es ein Gewitter geben?
*wirt es yn ge-**vit**-er gayb-en*

Isn't it a lovely day?
Ist es nicht ein wunderschöner Tag?
*ist es neekht yn **voond**-er-shoen-er **tag***

It has stopped snowing
Es hat aufgehört zu schneien
*es hat **owf**-ge-hoert tsoo **shny**-en*

It is a very clear night
Es ist eine sehr klare Nacht
*es ist yn-e **zayr** klar-e **nakht***

It is far too hot
Es ist viel zu heiß
*es ist **veel** tsoo **hys***

It is foggy
Es ist neblig
*es ist **nay**-bel-eekh*

The weather

It is going — to be fine
  Es wird — schön
    es virt — shoen

        — to be windy
        — windig
        —vind-eekh

        — to rain
        — regnen
        —rayg-nen

        — to snow
        — schneien
        —shny-en

It is raining again
Es regnet wieder
es rayg-net veed-er

It is very cold
Es ist sehr kalt
es ist zayr kalt

It is very windy
Es ist sehr windig
es ist zayr vind-eekh

There is a cool breeze
Es geht ein kühler Wind
es gayt yn kûl-er vint

What is the temperature?
Welche Temperatur haben wir?
velkh-e tem-per-a-toor hab-en veer

The weather

Will it be cold tonight?
Wird es heute nacht kalt werden?
*virt es **hoyt**-e **nakht** kalt vayr-den*

Will the weather improve?
Wird das Wetter besser werden?
*virt das **vet**-er bes-er **vayrd**-en*

Will the wind die down?
Wird sich der Wind legen?
*virt zeekh der **vint** layg-en*

On the beach

Can you recommend a quiet beach?
Können Sie einen ruhigen Strand empfehlen?
*koen-en zee yn-en **roo**-eeg-en **shtrant** emp-**fayl**-en*

Is it safe to swim here?
Kann man hier unbesorgt schwimmen?
*kan man heer **oon**-be-zorgt **shvim**-en*

Is the current strong?
Ist die Strömung stark?
*ist dee **stroem**-oong **shtark***

Is the sea calm?
Ist das Meer ruhig?
*ist das **mayr roo**-eekh*

Is the water warm?
Ist das Wasser warm?
*ist das **vas**-er **varm***

On the beach

Is there a lifeguard here?
Gibt es hier einen Bademeister?
*gipt es heer yn-en **bad**-e-myst-er*

Can we change here?
Können wir uns hier umziehen?
***koen**-en veer oons heer **oom**-tsee-en*

Is it possible to go — sailing?
    Kann man hier — segeln — gehen?
    ***kan** man heer —**sayg**-eln gay-en*

        — surfing?
        — Wellenreiten?
        *—**vel**-en-ryt-en*

        — water skiing?
        — Wasserski fahren?
        *—**vas**-er-shee-far-en*

        — wind surfing?
        — Windsurfen
        *—**vint**-surf-en*

Is this beach private?
Ist das ein Privatstrand?
*ist das yn pree-**vat**-shtrant*

When is high tide?
Wann ist Flut?
*van ist **floot***

When is low tide?
Wann ist Ebbe?
*van ist **eb**-e*

Sport and recreation

Is there a heated swimming pool?
Haben Sie ein beheiztes Schwimmbecken?
*hab-en zee yn be-**hytst**-es **shvim**-bek-en*

Can I rent — a sailing boat?
  Kann ich — ein Segelboot — mieten?
  *kan eekh —yn **zayg**-el-boat **meet**-en*

          — a rowing boat?
          — ein Ruderboot?
          *—yn **rood**-er-boat*

Can I rent the equipment?
Kann ich die Ausrüstung mieten?
*kan eekh dee **ows**-rûst-oong **meet**-en*

      Can we — play tennis?
  Können wir — Tennis spielen?
  ***koen**-en veer —**te**-nees **shpeel**-en*

          — play golf?
          — Golf spielen?
          *—golf **shpeel**-en*

          — play volleyball?
          — Volleyball spielen?
          *—**vo**-lay-bal **shpeel**-en*

Can we go riding?
Können wir Reiten gehen?
***koen**-en veer **ryt**-en **gay**-en*

Entertainment

Where can we fish?
Wo können wir fischen?
voa koen-en veer fish-en

Do we need a permit?
Brauchen wir eine Lizenz?
browkh-en veer yn-e lee-tsents

Entertainment

Is there — a disco?
Gibt es hier — eine Disco?
gipt es heer —yn-e disk-oa

> **— a casino?**
> — ein Kasino?
> *— yn ka-see-noa*

> **— a theatre?**
> — ein Theater?
> *— yn tay-a-ter*

> **— a good nightclub?**
> — einen guten Nachtclub?
> *— yn-en goot-en nakht-kloob*

Are there any films in English?
Werden hier auch englische Filme gezeigt?
vayrd-en heer owkh eng-leesh-e film-e ge-tsygt

How much is it per person?
Wieviel kostet es pro Person?
vee-feel kost-et es pro per-zoan

Entertainment

How much is it to get in?
Wieviel kostet es hineinzugehen?
vee-feel kost-et es heen-yn-tsoo -gay-en

Is there a reduction for children?
Gibt es eine Ermäßigung für Kinder?
gipt es yn-e er-mes-eeg-oong für kind-er

Two stall tickets, please
Zwei Karten für Sperrsitze, bitte
tsvy kart-en für shper-sits-e bit-e

Two tickets, please
Zwei Karten, bitte
tsvy kart-en bit-e

Sightseeing

Are there any boat trips on the river?
Gibt es Bootsfahrten auf dem Fluß?
gipt es boats-fart-en owf dem floos

Are there any guided tours of the castle?
Gibt es Führungen durch die Burg?
gipt es für-oong-en doorkh dee boorg

Are there any guided tours?
Gibt es Führungen?
gipt es für-oong-en

Is there a tour of the cathedral?
Gibt es eine Führung durch den Dom?
gipt es yn-e für-oong doorkh den doam

Sightseeing

Is there an English-speaking guide?
Haben Sie einen Englisch sprechenden Führer?
hab-en zee yn-en eng-leesh shprekh-end-en fûr-er

How long does the tour take?
Wie lange dauert die Rundfahrt?
vee lang-e dow-ert dee roont-fart

When is the bus tour?
Wann findet die Busrundfahrt statt?
van find-et dee boos-roont-fart shtat

What is there to see here?
Was gibt es hier zu sehen?
vas gipt es heer tsoo zay-en

What is this building?
Welch ein Gebäude ist das?
velkh yn ge-boyd-e ist das

When was it built?
Wann wurde es gebaut?
van voord-e es ge-bowt

Can we go in?
Können wir hineingehen?
koen-en veer heen-yn-gay-en

Is it open to the public?
Ist es für die Öffentlichkeit zu betreten?
ist es fûr dee oef-ent-leekh-kyt tsoo be-trayt-en

Is there a guidebook?
Haben Sie einen Ortsführer?
hab-en zee yn-en orts-fûr-er

Entertainment

What is the admission charge?
Was kostet der Eintritt?
*vas **kost**-et der **yn**-tritt*

How much is it for a child?
Wieviel kostet es für ein Kind?
*vee-feel **kost**-et es für yn **kint***

When is the bus tour?
Wann findet die Busrundfahrt statt?
*van **find**-et dee **boos**-roont-fart **shtat***

Can we go up to the top?
Können wir nach oben gehen?
***koen**-en veer nakh **oab**-en gay-en*

Is this the best view?
Ist das die beste Aussicht?
*ist das dee **best**-e **ows**-zeekht*

What time does the gallery open?
Wann öffnet die Galerie?
*van **oef**-net dee gal-e-**ree***

Can I take photos?
Können wir Fotos machen?
***koen**-en veer **foa**-toas **makh**-en*

Can I use flash?
Kann ich mein Blitzlicht verwenden?
*kan eekh myn **blits**-leekht fer-**vend**-en*

Souvenirs

Where can I buy postcards?
Wo kann ich Postkarten kaufen?
*voa kan eekh **post**-kart-en **kowf**-en*

Where can we buy souvenirs?
Wo kann ich Andenken kaufen?
*voa kan eekh **an**-denk-en **kowf**-en*

Have you got an English guidebook?
Haben Sie einen Führer in englischer Sprache?
***hab**-en zee yn-en **fûr**-er in **eng**-leesh-er **shprakh**-e*

Have you got any colour slides?
Haben Sie Farbdias?
***hab**-en zee **farb**-dee-as*

Going to church

I would like to see — a priest
      Ich möchte — einen Priester — sehen,
*eekh **moekht**-e —yn-en **preest**-er **zay**-en*

                — a minister
                — einen Pfarrer
                *—yn-en **pfar**-er*

                — a rabbi
                — einen Rabbiner
                *—yn-en ra-**been**-er*

Going to church

Where is the — Catholic church?
   Wo ist die — katholische Kirche?
   *voa ist dee —ka-**toal**-eesh-e **kirkh**-e*

                    — Baptist church?
                    — Baptistenkirche?
                    *—bap-**teest**-en-**kirkh**-e*

                    — mosque?
                    — Moschee?
                    *—mo-**shay***

                    — Protestant church?
                    — protestantische Kirche?
                    *—pro-test-**ant**-eesh-e **kirkh**-e*

                    — synagogue?
                    — Synagoge?
                    *—zû-na-**goag**-e*

What time is the service?
Wann findet der Gottesdienst statt?
*van find-et der **got**-es-deenst **shtat***

SHOPPING

General phrases and requests

How much is this?
Was macht das?
*vas **makht** das*

How much does that cost?
Was kostet das?
*vas **kost**-et das*

   How much is it — per kilo?
  Wieviel kostet es — pro Kilo?
*vee-feel **kost**-et es —pro **keel**-oa*

         — per metre?
         — pro Meter?
        *—pro **mayt**-er*

I like this one
Das gefällt mir
*das ge-**felt** meer*

I do not like it
Das gefällt mir nicht
*das ge-**felt** meer **neekht***

I will take that one
Ich nehmen das
*eekh **naym**-e das*

I will take the other one
Ich nehmen das andere
*eekh **naym**-e das **and**-er-e*

General phrases and requests

I will take this one
Ich nehmen dieses
*eekh **naym**-e deez-es*

No, the other one
Nein, das andere
*nyn das **and**-er-e*

Have you got anything cheaper?
Haben Sie etwas Billigeres?
***hab**-en zee et-vas **bil**-ig-er-es*

Can I have a carrier bag?
Könnte ich eine Tragetasche haben?
***koent**-e eekh yn-e **trag**-e-tash-e hab-en*

Can I pay for air insurance?
Kann ich gegen Gebühr eine Luftfrachtversicherung
abschließen?
*kan eekh gayg-en ge-**bûr** yn-e **looft**-frakht-fer-zeekh-er-oong
ap-shlees-en*

Can I see that one over there?
Könnte ich mir das da drüben ansehen?
***koent**-e eekh meer das da -**drûb**-en **an**-zay-en*

Can I see that umbrella?
Könnte ich mir diesen Schirm anschauen?
***koent**-e eekh meer deez-en **shirm an**-show-en*

Can you deliver to my hotel?
Können Sie es mir in meinem Hotel liefern?
***koen**-en zee es meer in myn-em hoa-**tel leef**-ern*

General phrases and requests

Do you sell sunglasses?
Verkaufen Sie Sonnenbrillen?
fer-kowf-en zee zon-en-bril-en

I am looking for a souvenir
Ich suche ein Andenken
eekh zookh-e yn an-denk-en

I do not have enough money
Ich habe nicht genug Geld
eekh hab-e neekht ge-noog- gelt

Please forward a receipt to this address
Bitte schicken Sie eine Rechnung an diese Adresse
bit-e shik-en zee yn-e rekh-noong an deez-e a-dres-e

Will you send it by air freight?
Schicken Sie es per Luftfracht?
shike-en zee es per looft-frakht

Please pack it for shipment
Bitte packen Sie das für den Transport ein
bit-e pak-en zee das fûr den trans-port yn

Please wrap it up for me
Bitte packen Sie es mir ein
bit-e pak-en zee es meer yn

There is no need to wrap it
Einzupacken ist nicht nötig
yn-tsoo-pak-en ist neekht noet-eekh

We need to buy some food
Wir müssen etwas zu essen kaufen
veer mûs-en et-vas tsoo es-en kowf-en

General phrases and requests

What is the total?
Was macht das zusammen?
*vas **macht** das tsoo-**zam**-en*

Where can I buy some clothes?
Wo kann ich Kleider kaufen?
*voa kan eekh **klyd**-er **kowf**-en*

Where can I buy cassette tapes and compact discs?
Wo kann ich Tonbandkassetten und Compact Disks
kaufen?
*voa kan eekh **toan**-bant-ka-**set**-en oont kom-**pakt** disks
kowf-en*

Where can I buy tapes for my camcorder?
Wo kann ich Kassetten für meinen Camcorder kaufen?
*voa kan eekh ka-**set**-en fûr myn-en **kam**-kord-er **kowf**-en*

Where can I get my camcorder repaired?
Wo kann ich meinen Camcorder reparieren lassen?
*voa kan eekh myn-en **kam**-kord-er re-pa-**reer**-en las-en*

Where is the children's department?
Wo ist die Kinderabteilung?
*voa ist dee **kind**-er-ap-tyl-oong*

Where is the the food department?
Wo ist die Lebensmittelabteilung?
*voa ist dee **layb**-ens-mit-el-**ab**-tyl-oong*

Buying groceries

Can I please have — some sugar?
   Kann ich bitte — etwas Zucker — haben?
   ***kan** eekh bit-e — et-vas **tsook**-er — **hab**-en*

> **— a bottle of wine?**
> — eine Flasche Wein?
> *—yn-e flash-e **vyn***

> **— a kilo of sausages?**
> — ein Kilo Würste?
> *—yn keel-oa **vûrst**-e*

> **— a leg of lamb?**
> — eine Lammshaxe?
> *—yn-e **lams**-haks-e*

> **— a litre of milk?**
> — einen Liter Milch?
> *—yn-en leet-er **milkh***

> **— two steaks?**
> — zwei Steaks?
> *—tsvy **stayks***

> **— a kilo of potatoes?**
> — ein Kilo Kartoffeln?
> *—yn **keel**-oa kar-tof-eln*

> **— a bar of chocolate?**
> — eine Tafel Schokolade?
> *—yn-e **taf**-el shok-oa-**lad**-e*

Buying groceries

Can I please have — 5 slices of ham?
Kann ich bitte — fünf Scheiben Schinken — haben?
kan eekh bit-e — fûnf shyb-en shink-en — hab-en

— 100 grams of ground coffee?
— hundert Gramm gemahlenen Kaffee?
— hoond-ert gram ge-mal-en-en ka-fay?

— half a dozen eggs?
— ein halbes Dutzend Eier?
— yn halb-es doots-ent y-er?

— half a kilo of butter?
— ein halbes Kilo Butter?
— yn halb-es keel-oa boot-er?

Groceries

baby food Babynahrung *bayb-ee-nar-oong*	**cheese** Käse *kez-e*
biscuits Plätzchen *plets-khen*	**coffee** Kaffee *ka-fay*
bread Brot *broat*	**cream** Sahne *zan-e*
butter Butter *boot-er*	**eggs** Eier *y-er*

flour
Mehl
mayl

groceries
Lebensmittel
layb-enz-mit-el

jam
Marmelade
mar-me-lad-e

margarine
Margarine
mar-ga-reen-e

milk
Milch
milkh

mustard
Senf
zenf

oil
Öl
oel

pasta
Nudeln
nood-eln

pepper
Pfeffer
pfef-er

rice
Reis
rys

salt
Salz
zalts

soup
Suppe
zoop-e

sugar
Zucker
tsook-er

tea
Tee
tay

vinegar
Essig
es-eekh

yoghurt
Joghurt
yoa-goort

Meat and fish

Meat and fish

beef
Rindfleisch
rint-flysh

chicken
Huhn
hoon

cod
Kabeljau
kab-el-yow

fish
Fisch
fish

hake
Hecht
hekht

ham
Schinken
shink-en

herring
Hering
hayr-ing

kidneys
Nieren
neer-en

lamb
Lamm
lam

liver
Leber
layb-er

meat
Fleisch
flysh

mussels
Muscheln
moosh-eln

pork
Schweinefleisch
shvyn-e-flysh

sole
Seezunge
zay-tsoong-e

tuna
Thunfisch
toon-fish

veal
Kalbsfleisch
kalps-flysh

At the newsagent's

Do you have — English newspapers?
  Haben Sie — englische Zeitungen?
  hab-en zee — eng-leesh-e tsyt-oong-en

          — English books?
          — englische Bücher?
          — eng-leesh-e bûkh-er

          — postcards?
          — Postkarten?
          — post-kart-en

Do you sell — English paperbacks?
  Verkaufen Sie — englische Taschenbücher?
  fer-kowf-en zee — eng-leesh-e tash-en-bûkh-er

          — coloured pencils?
          — Farbstifte?
          —farb-shtift-e

          — drawing paper?
          — Zeichenpapier?
          —tsykh-en-pa-peer

          — felt pens?
          — Filzschreiber?
          —filts-shryb-er

          — street maps?
          — Straßenkarten?
          —shtras-en-kart-en

At the newsagent's

I would like — some postage stamps
Ich hätte gerne — ein paar Briefmarken
*eekh het-e gern-e — yn par **breef**-mark-en*

> **— a bottle of ink**
> — einen Behälter mit Tinte
> *— yn-en be-**helt**-er mit **tint**-e*

> **— a pen**
> — einen Federhalter
> *— yn-en **fayd**-er-halt-er*

> **— a pencil**
> — einen Bleistift
> *— yn-en **bly**-shtift*

> **— some adhesive tape**
> — etwas Klebstreifen
> *— etvas **klayb**-shtryf-en*

> **— some envelopes**
> — Umschläge
> *— **oom**-shleg-e*

I need — some note paper
Ich brauche — Schreibpapier
*eekh **browkh**-e — **shryb**-pa-peer*

> **— a local map**
> — eine Karte des Ortes
> *— yn-e **kart**-e des **ort**-es*

> **— a road map**
> — eine Straßenkarte
> *— yn-e **shtras**-en-kart-e*

At the tobacconist's

I would like — a box of matches
Ich hätte gerne — eine Packung Streichhölzer
eekh het-e gern-e —yn-e pak-oong shtrykh-hoelts-er

> **— a cigar**
> — eine Zigarre
> *—yn-e tsee-gar-e*

> **— a cigarette lighter**
> — ein Feuerzeug
> *—yn foy-er-tsoyg*

> **— a gas (butane) refill**
> — eine Nachfüllpackung Butangas
> *—yn-e nakh-fûl-pak-oong boo-tan-gas*

> **— a pipe**
> — eine Pfeife
> *—yn-e pfyf-e*

> **— a pouch of pipe tobacco**
> — ein Päckchen Pfeifentabak
> *—yn pek-khen pfyf-en-ta-bak*

> **— some pipe cleaners**
> — ein paar Pfeifenreiniger
> *—yn par pfyf-en-ryn-eeg-er*

Do you have cigarette papers?
Haben Sie Zigarettenpapier?
hab-en zee tsee-ga-ret-en-pa-peer

At the tobacconist's

Do you have rolling tobacco?
Haben Sie Tabak zum Selberdrehen?
hab-en zee ta-bak tsoom zelb-er-dray-en

Have you got any American brands?
Führen Sie amerikanische Marken?
fûr-en zee a-may-ree-kan-eesh-e mark-en

Have you got any English brands?
Führen Sie englische Marken?
fûr-en zee eng-leesh-e mark-en

A packet of ... please
Bitte eine Packung ...
bit-e yn-e pak-oong...

— with filter tips
— mit Filter
—mit filt-er

— without filters
— ohne Filter
—oan-e filt-er

At the chemist's

I need some high-protection suntan cream
Ich brauche Sonnencreme mit hohem Schutzfaktor
eekh browkh-e zon-en-kraym-e mit hoa-em shoots-fak-tor

I need some antibiotics
Ich brauche Antibiotika
eekh browkh-e an-tee-bee-o-tee-ka

At the chemist's

Can you give me something for— a headache?
   Können Sie mir etwas gegen — Kopfschmerzen geben?
   koen-en zee meer et-vas gayg-en — kopf-shmerts-en gayb-en

          — a cold?
          — eine Erkältung?
          —yn-e er-kelt-oong

          — a cough?
          — Husten?
          — hoost-en

          — a sore throat?
          — Halsentzündung?
          — hals-ent-tsûnd-oong

          — an upset stomach?
          — eine Magenverstimmung?
          —yn-e mag-en-fer-shtim-oong

          — sunburn?
          — Sonnenbrand?
          — zon-en-brant

          — chapped lips?
          — aufgesprungene Lippen?
          — owf-ge-shproong-en-e lip-en

          — swollen feet?
          — geschwollene Füße?
          — ge-shvol-en-e fûs-e

          — toothache?
          — Zahnschmerzen?
          — tsan-shmerts-en

At the chemist's

Can you give me something for insect bites?
Können Sie mir etwas gegen Insektenstiche geben?
koen-en zee meer et-vas gayg-en in-zekt-en-shtikh-e gayb-en

Do I need a prescription?
Brauche ich dafür ein Rezept?
browkh-e eekh da-für yn re-tsept

How many do I take?
Wieviel nehme ich davon?
vee-feel naym-e eekh da-fon

How often do I take them?
Wie oft nehme ich sie?
vee oft naym-e eekh zee

Are they safe for children to take?
Können sie auch bedenkenlos Kindern gegeben werden?
koen-en zee owkh be-denk-en-loas kind-ern ge-gayb-en vayrd-en

Do you have toothpaste?
Haben Sie Zahnpasta?
hab-en zee tsan-past-a

Medicines and toiletries

aftershave
Rasierwasser
ra-zeer-vas-er

antihistamine
Antihistamin
ant-ee-his-ta-meen

antiseptic
Antiseptikum
ant-ee-zep-tee-koom

aspirin
Aspirin
as-pee-reen

Medicines and toiletries

Band-aid
Pflaster
pflast-er

bandage
Verband
fer-bant

bubble bath
Schaumbad
showm-bat

cleansing milk
Reinigungsmilch
ryn-ee-goongs-milkh

contraceptive
Empfängnisverhütungsmittel
emp-feng-nis-fer-hût-oongs-mit-el

cotton wool
Watte
vat-e

deodorant
Deodorant
day-oad-oa-rant

disinfectant
Desinfektionsmittel
dayz-in-fek-tsee-oans-mit-el

eau de Cologne
Eau de Cologne
oa de ko-lon-ye

eye shadow
Lidschatten
lid-shat-en

hair spray
Haarspray
har-shpray

hand cream
Handcreme
hant-kraym

hay fever
Heuschnupfen
hoy-shnup-fen

insect repellent
Insektenspray
in-zekt-en-shpray

Kleenex
Tempo
temp-oa

laxative
Abführmittel
ap-fûr-mit-el

lipstick
Lippenstift
lip-en-shtift

mascara
Maskara
mas-ka-ra

Medicines and toiletries

mouthwash
Mundspülung
moont-shpûl-oong

nail file
Nagelfeile
nag-el-fyl-e

nail varnish
Nagellack
nag-el-lak

nail varnish remover
Nagellackentferner
nag-el-lak-ent-fern-er

perfume
Parfüm
par-fûm

powder
Puder
pood-er

razor blades
Rasierklingen
ra-zeer-kling-en

sanitary towels
(Hygiene)binden
(hûg-ee-ayn-e) bind-en

shampoo
Haarshampoo
haar-sham-poo

shaving cream
Rasiercreme
ra-zeer-kraym

skin moisturiser
Feuchtigkeitscreme
foykht-eekh-kyts-kraym

soap
Seife
zyf-e

suntan oil
Sonnenöl
zon-en-oel

talc
Puder
pood-er

toilet water
Eau de Toilette
oa de twa-let

toothpaste
Zahnpasta
tsan-past-a

Shopping for clothes

I am just looking, thank you
Danke, ich schaue mich nur um
dank-e eekh show-e meekh noor oom

I like it
Es gefällt mir
es ge-felt meer

I do not like it
Es gefällt mir nicht
es ge-felt meer neekht

I would like — this hat
Ich hätte gerne — diesen Hut
eekh het-e gern-e — deez-en hoot

— this suit
— diesen Anzug
— deez-en an-tsoog

I like — this one
Mir gefällt — dieses
meer ge-felt — deez-es

— that one there
— das da
— das da

— the one in the window
— das im Fenster
— das im fenst-er

Shopping for clothes

I will take it
Ich nehme es
*eekh **naym**-e es*

Can I change it if it does not fit?
Kann ich es umtauschen, falls es nicht paßt?
kan** eekh es **oom**-towsh-en fals es neekht **past

Can you please measure me?
Können Sie mich bitte messen?
***koen**-en zee meekh bit-e **mes**-en*

I take continental size 40
In Europa brauche ich Größe 40
*in **roa**-pa browkh-e eekh **groes**-e **feer**-tseekh*

   Have you got — a large size?
   Haben Sie eine — größere Größe
   ***hab**-en zee yn-e — **groes**-er-e **groes**-e*

                  — a smaller size?
                  — kleinere Größe
                  *— **klyn**-er-e **groes**-e*

Have you got this in other colours?
Haben Sie das auch in anderen Farben?
***hab**-en zee das owkh in **and**-er-en **farb**-en*

Where are the changing (dressing) rooms?
Wo sind die Umkleidekabinen?
***voa** zind dee **oom**-klyd-e-ka-**been**-en*

Where can I try it on?
Wo kann ich es anprobieren?
***voa** kan eekh es **an**-pro-beer-en*

Shopping for clothes

Is there a full-length mirror?
Gibt es hier einen großen Spiegel?
*gipt es heer yn-en **groas**-en **shpeeg**-el*

May I see it in daylight?
Kann ich das im Tageslicht anschauen?
*kan eekh das im **tag**-es-likht **an**-show-en*

It does not fit
Es paßt nicht
*es **past** neekht*

Is it too long?
Ist es zu lang?
*ist es tsoo **lang***

Is it too short?
Ist es zu kurz?
*ist es tsoo **koorts***

Is this all you have?
Ist das alles, was Sie haben?
*ist das **al**-es vas zee **hab**-en*

It does not suit me
Es paßt nicht zu mir
*es **past** neekht tsoo meer*

I would like one — with a zip
Ich hätte gerne eines — mit Reißverschluß
*eekh **het**-e gern-e yn-es —mit **rys**-fer-shloos*

— without a belt
— ohne Gürtel
*—oan-e **gûrt**-e*

Shopping for clothes

Is it guaranteed?
Gibt es dafür eine Garantie?
gipt es da-für yn-e ga-ran-tee

What is it made of?
Woraus besteht das?
voa-rows be-shtayt das

Is it drip-dry?
Darf man es nicht schleudern?
darf man es neekht shloyd-ern

Is it dry-clean only?
Muß man es chemisch reinigen?
moos man es khaym-eesh ryn-ee-gen

Is it machine-washable?
Kann ich es in der Maschine waschen?
kan eekh es in der mas-sheen-e vash-en

Will it shrink?
Geht es ein?
gayt es ynl

Clothes and accessories

acrylic
Acryl
a-krül

blouse
Bluse
blooz-e

belt
Gürtel
gürt-el

bra
BH
bay-ha

Clothes and accessories

bracelet
Armband
arm-bant

brooch
Brosche
broash-e

button
Knopf
knopf

cardigan
Strickjacke
shtrik-yak-e

coat
Mantel
mant-el

corduroy
Cord
kord

denim
Jeansstoff
jeens-shtof

dress
Kleid
klyt

dungarees
Latzhose
lats-hoaz-e

earrings
Ohrringe
oar-ring-e

fur
Pelz
pelts

gloves
Handschuhe
hant-shoo-e

handbag
Handtasche
hant-tash-e

handkerchief
Taschentuch
-*en-tookh*

hat
Hut
hoot

jacket
Jacke
yak-e

jeans
Jeans
jeenz

jersey
Pulli
pool-ee

Clothes and accessories

lace
Spitze
shpits-e

leather
Leder
layd-er

linen
Leinen
lyn-en

necklace
Halsband
hals-bant

night-dress
Nachthemd
nakht-hemt

nylon
Nylon
ny-lon

panties
Unterhosen
oont-er-hoaz-en

pendant
Anhänger
an-heng-er

petticoat
Unterrock
oont-er-rok

polyester
Polyester
pol-ee-est-er

poplin
Popeline
pop-e-leen-e

pullover
Pullover
pool-oaf-er

purse
Geldbeutel
gelt-boyt-el

pyjamas
Schlafanzug
shlaf-an-tsoog

raincoat
Regenmantel
rayg-en-mant-el

rayon
Kunstseide/Rayon
koonst-zyd-e/ray-on

ring
Ring
ring

sandals
Sandalen
zan-dal-en

Clothes and accessories

scarf
Schal
shal

shirt
Hemd
hemt

shorts
kurze Hosen
koorts-e hoaz-en

silk
Seide
zyd-e

skirt
Rock
rok

slip
Unterrock
oont-er-rok

socks
Socken
zok-en

stockings
lange Strümpfe
lang-e shtrûmpf-e

suede
Wildleder
vilt-layd-er

suit (men's)
Anzug
an-tsoog

suit (women's)
Kostüm
kos-tûm

sweater
Pullover
pool-oaf-er

swimming trunks
Badehose
bad-e-hoaz-e

swimsuit
Badeanzug
bad-e-an-tsoog

T-shirt
T-shirt
tee-shirt

terylene
Terylen
ter-ee-layn

tie
Krawatte
kra-vat-e

tights
Strumpfhose
shtroompf-hoaz-e

Clothes and accessories

towel
Handtuch
hant-tookh

vest
Unterhemd
oont-er-hemt

trousers
Hose
hoaz-e

wallet
Brieftasche
breef-tash-e

umbrella
Schirm
shirm

watch
Armbanduhr
arm-bant-oor

underpants
Unterhose
unt-er-hoaz-e

wool
Wolle
vol-e

velvet
Samt
zamt

zip
Reißverschluß
rys-fer-shloos

Photography

Can you develop this film, please?
Könnten Sie bitte diesen Film entwickeln?
koent-en zee bit-e deez-en film ent-vik-eln

I would like this photo enlarged
Ich hätte dieses Foto gerne vergrößert
eekh het-e deez-es foa-toa gern-e fer-groes-ert

I would like two prints of this one
Ich hätte gerne zwei Abzüge davon
eekh het-e gern-e tsvy ap-tsûg-e da-fon

Camera parts

cassette
Kassette
ka-set-e

cine camera
Filmkamera
film-ka-me-ra

distance
Entfernung
ent-fern-oong

enlargement
Vergrößerung
fer-groes-er-oong

exposure
Belichtung
be-leekht-oong

exposure meter
Belichtungsmesser
be-leekht-oongs-mes-er

flash
Blitz
blits

flash bulb
Blitzlichtbirne
blits-leekht-birn-e

flash cube
Blitzlichtwürfel
blits-leekht-vûrf-el

focal distance
Entfernung
ent-fern-oong

focus
Brennpunkt
bren-poonkt

image
Abbildung
ap-bild-oong

in focus
scharf eingestellt
sharf yn-ge-shtelt

lens cover
Linsendeckel
linz-en-dek-el

lens
Linse
linz-e

negative
Negativ
nay-ga-teef

out of focus
nicht scharf eingestellt
neekht sharf yn-ge-stelt

over-exposed
zu stark belichtet
tsoo shtark be-leekht-et

Camera parts

picture
Bild
bilt

print
Papierbild
pa-peer-bilt

projector
Projektor
proa-yek-tor

red filter
Rotfilter
roat-filt-er

reel
Spule
shpool-e

rewind mechanism
Rückspulmechanismus
rûk-shpool-may-kha-neez-moos

shade
Schatten
shat-en

shutter
Blende
blend-e

shutter speed
Belichtungszeit
be-leekht-oongs-tsyt

slide
Dia
dee-a

transparency
Transparenz
trans-pa-rents

tripod
Stativ
shta-teef

under-exposed
zu wenig belichtet
tsoo vayn-eekh be-leekht-et

viewfinder
Sucher
zookh-er

wide-angle lens
Weitwinkelobjektiv
vyt-vink-el-ob-yek-teef

yellow filter
Gelbfilter
gelp-filt-er

At the hairdresser's

I would like to make an appointment
Ich möchte mich anmelden
*eekh **moekht**-e meekh **an**-meld-en*

  I would like — a perm
  Ich hätte gerne — eine Dauerwelle
  *eekh **het**-e gern-e —yn-e **dow**-er-vel-e*

              — a blow-dry
              — Föhnen
              *—**foen**-en*

              — my hair dyed
              — Haare Färben
              *—**har**-e ferb-en*

              — my hair streaked
              — Strähnchen
              *—**stren**-khen*

              — shampoo and cut
              — Waschen und Schneiden
              *—**vash**-en oont **shnyd**-en*

              — shampoo and set
              — Waschen und Legen
              *—**vash**-en oont **layg**-en*

I want a haircut
Ich möchte meine Haare schneiden lassen
*eekh **moekht**-e myn-e **har**-e shnyd-en **las**-en*

At the hairdresser's

I want a trim
Ich möchte meine Haare nachschneiden lassen
eekh moekht-e myn-e har-e nakh-shnyd-en las-en

Please cut my hair — short
Schneiden Sie meine Haare bitte — kurz
shnyd-en zee myn-e har-e bit-e — koorts

— fairly short
— ziemlich kurz
—tseem-leekh koorts

— in a fringe
— zu einem Pony
—tsoo yn-em poan-ee

— not too short
— nicht allzu kurz
—neekht al-tsoo koorts

Take a little more off the back
Schneiden Sie hinten bitte noch etwas weg
shnyd-en zee hint-en bit-e nokh et-vas vek

Not too much off
Nicht zu viel weg
neekht tsoo feel vek

I would like — a conditioner
Ich hätte gerne — Conditioner
eekh het-e gern-e —kon-dish-en-er

— hair spray
— Haarspray
—har-shpray

That is fine, thank you
Das ist gut so, danke
*das ist **goot** zoa **dank**-e*

The dryer is too hot
Die Trockenhaube ist zu heiß
*dee **trok**-en-howb-e ist tsoo **hys***

The water is too hot
Das Wasser ist zu heiß
*das **vas**-er ist tsoo **hys***

Laundry

Is there a launderette nearby?
Gibt es in der Nähe einen Waschsalon?
*gipt es in der **ne**-e yn-en **vash**-za-loan*

How does the machine work?
Wie funktioniert dieses Gerät?
*vee foonk-tsee-o-**neert** deez-es ge-**ret***

How long will it take?
Wie lange dauert das?
*vee lang-e **dow**-ert das*

I will come back in an hour
Ich komme in einer Stunde
*eekh **kom**-e in yn-er **shtoond**-e*

What time do you close?
Wann schließen Sie?
*van **shlees**-en zee*

Laundry

Can you — clean this skirt?
Können Sie — diesen Rock reinigen?
koen-en zee — deez-en rok ryn-ee-gen

> **— clean and press these shirts?**
> — diese Hemden reinigen und bügeln?
> *— deez-e hemd-en ryn-ee-gen oont bûg-eln*

> **— wash these clothes?**
> — diese Kleider waschen?
> *— deez-e klyd-er vash-en*

This stain is — oil
Das ist ein — Ölfleck
das ist yn — oel-flek

> **— blood**
> — Blutfleck
> *— bloot-flek*

> **— coffee**
> — Kaffeefleck
> *— ka-fay-flek*

> **— ink**
> — Tintenfleck
> *— tint-en-flek*

I will come back later
Ich komme später zurück
eekh kom-e shpet-er tsoo-rûk

When will I come back?
Wann soll ich zurückkommen?
van zol eekh tsoo-rûk-kom-en

General repairs

When will my things be ready?
Wann sind meine Sachen fertig?
*van zint myn-e zakh-en **fert**-eekh*

Can you do it quickly?
Können Sie es schnell machen?
***koen**-en zee es **shnel** makh-en*

Please send it to this address
Bitte schicken Sie es an diese Adresse
*bit-e **shik**-en zee es an deez-e a-**dres**-e*

General repairs

This is — broken
Das ist — kaputt
*das ist — ka-**poot***

> **— damaged**
> — beschädigt
> *— be-**shed**-eekht*

> **— torn**
> — zerrissen
> *— tser-**ris**-en*

Can you repair it?
Können Sie es reparieren?
***koen**-en zee es re-pa-**reer**-en*

Have you got a spare part for this?
Haben Sie ein Ersatzteil dafür?
hab**-en zee yn er-**zats**-tyl da-**für

General repairs

Would you have a look at this please?
Könnten Sie sich das bitte einmal anschauen?
*koent-en zee zeekh das bit-e yn-mal **an**-show-en*

Here is the guarantee
Hier ist die Garantie
heer** ist dee ga-ran-**tee

I need new heels on these shoes
Ich brauche an diesen Schuhen neue Absätze
*eekh **browkh**-e an deez-en **shoo**-en noy-e **ap**-zets-e*

At the Post Office

12 stamps please
zwölf Briefmarken bitte
*tsvoelf **breef**-mark-en **bit**-e*

Can I have a telegram form, please?
Könnte ich bitte einen Telegrammvordruck haben?
*koent-e eekh **bit**-e yn-en tay-lay-**gram**-foar-drook **hab**-en*

I need to send this by courier
Ich muß das per Kurier schicken
*eekh **moos** das per koo-**reer** shik-en*

I want to send a telegram
Ich möchte ein Telegramm schicken
*eekh **moekht**-e yn tay-lay-**gram** shik-en*

I want to send this by registered mail
Ich möchte das per Einschreiben schicken
*eekh **moekht**-e das per **yn**-shryb-en **shik**-en*

Using the telephone

I want to send this parcel
Ich möchte dieses Paket abschicken
eekh moekht-e deez-es pa-kayt ap-shik-en

When will it arrive?
Wann wird es ankommen?
van virt es an-kom-en

How much is a letter — to Britain?
Wieviel kostet ein Brief — nach Großbritannien?
vee-feel kost-et yn breef — nakh groas-bri-tan-ee-en

— to the United States?
— in die Vereinigten Staaten
— in dee fer-yn-eeg-ten shtat-en

Can I have six stamps for postcards to Britain?
Kann ich bitte sechs Briefmarken für Postkarten nach
Großbritannien haben?
*kan eekh bit-e zeks breef-mark-en fûr post-kart-en nakh
gros-bri-tan-ee-en hab-en*

Using the telephone

Can I use the telephone, please?
Kann ich bitte das Telefon benutzen?
kan eekh bit-e das tay-lay-foan be-noots-en

Can you connect me with the international operator?
Könnten Sie mich bitte mit der internationalen
Telefonvermittlung verbinden?
*koent-en zee meekh bit-e mit der in-ter-na-tsee-oa-nal-en
tay-lay-foan-fer-mit-loong fer-bind-en*

Using the telephone

Can I dial direct?
Kann ich direkt wählen?
*kan eekh dee-**rekt** vel-en*

How do I use the telephone?
Wie verwendet man dieses Telefon?
*vee fer-**vend**-et man deez-es **tay**-lay-foan*

I must make a phone call to Britain
Ich muß mit Großbritannien telefonieren
*eekh **moos** mit groas-bri-**tan**-ee-en tay-lay-fo-**neer**-en*

I need to make a phone call
Ich muß telefonieren
*eekh moos tay-lay-fo-**neer**-en*

The number I need is...
Die Nummer, die ich brauche, lautet...
*dee **noom**-er dee eekh **browkh**-e **lowt**-et...*

How much is it to phone to London?
Wieviel kostet es nach London anzurufen?
*vee-feel **kost**-et es nakh **lon**-don **an**-tsoo-roof-en*

What is the charge?
Was kostet das?
*vas **kost**-et das*

Please, call me back
Bitte rufen Sie mich zurück
*bit-e **roof**-en zee meekh tsoo-**rûk***

I am sorry. We were cut off
Es tut mir leid. Die Leitung wurde unterbrochen
*es toot meer **lyt** dee **lyt**-oong voord-e oont-er-**brokh**-en*

Using the telephone

I would like to make a reversed charge call
Ich möchte gerne einen vom Empfänger bezahlten Anruf
machen
*eekh moekht-e gern-e yn-en fom emp-**feng**-er be-**tsalt**-en
an-roof makh-en*

What is the code for the UK?
Was ist die Vorwahl für Großbritannien?
*vas ist dee **foar**-val für gros-bri-**tan**-ee-en*

Bitte, tun Sie das
Please go ahead
*bit-e **toon** zee das*

Die Leitung ist belegt
The line is engaged
*dee **lyt**-oong ist be-**laygt***

Die Nummer funktioniert nicht
The number is out of order
*dee **noom**-er foonk-tsee-o-**neert** neekht*

Ich komme bei dieser Nummer nicht durch
I cannot obtain this number
*eekh **kom**-e by deez-er **noom**-eer neekht **doorkh***

Ich stelle Sie an Herrn Smith durch
I am putting you through to Mr Smith
*eekh **stel**-e zee an hern **smith** doorkh*

Ich versuche, Sie zu verbinden
I am trying to connect you
*eekh fer-**zookh**-e zee tsoo fer-**bind**-en*

Changing money

Changing money

Can I contact my bank to arrange for a transfer?
Kann ich mich mit meiner Bank über die Regelung einer
Überweisung in Verbindung setzen?
*kan eekh meekh mit myn-er **bank** ûb-er dee **rayg**-el-oong
yn-er ûb-er-vyz-oong in fer-**bind**-oong **zets**-en*

I would like to obtain a cash advance with my credit card
Ich hätte gerne eine Bargeldauszahlung auf meine
Kreditkarte
*eekh **het**-e gern-e yn-e **bar**-gelt-ows-tsal-oong owf myn-e
kray-**deet**-kart-e*

Has my cash arrived?
Ist mein Geld angekommen?
*ist myn **gelt** an-ge-kom-en*

Here is my passport
Hier ist mein Paß
*__heer__ ist myn **pas***

I would like to cash a cheque with my Eurocheque card
Ich möchte gerne mit meiner Eurocheque-Karte einen
Scheck einlösen
*eekh **moekht**-e gern-e mit myn-er **oy**-roa-shek-kart-e yn-en
shek yn-**loez**-en*

This is the name and address of my bank
Das sind Name und Adresse meiner Bank
*das zint **nam**-e oont a-**dres**-e myn-er **bank***

Changing money

What is the rate of exchange?
Was ist der Wechselkurs?
*vas ist der **veks**-el-koors*

What is your commission?
Wie hoch ist Ihre Kommission?
*vee **hoakh** ist eer-e ko-mee-see-oan*

Can I change — these traveller's cheques?
Kann ich — diese Reiseschecks — hier umtauschen?
***kan** eekh —deez-e **ryz**-e-sheks —heer **oom**-towsh-en*

— these notes?
— diese Banknoten?
*—deez-e **bank**-noat-en*

What is the rate for — sterling?
Was ist der gängige Kurs für — britische Pfund?
*vas ist der **geng**-eeg-e- **koors** für — **brit**-eesh-e **pfoont***

— dollars?
— Dollars?
*—**dol**-ars*

HEALTH

What's wrong?

I need a doctor
Ich brauche einen Arzt
*eekh **browkh**-e yn-en **artst***

Can I see a doctor?
Kann ich einen Arzt sehen?
***kan** eekh yn-en **artst** zay-en*

He has been badly injured
Er wurde schwer verletzt
*er voord-e **shvayr** fer-**letst***

He is unconscious
Er ist bewußtlos
*er ist be-**voost**-loas*

He has burnt himself
Er hat sich verbrannt
*er hat zeekh fer-**brant***

He has dislocated his shoulder
Er hat sich die Schulter verrenkt
*er hat zeekh dee **shoolt**-er fer-**renkt***

He is hurt
Er ist verletzt
*er ist fer-**letst***

My son is ill
Mein Sohn ist krank
*myn **zoan** ist **krank***

What's wrong?

I am a diabetic
Ich bin Diabetiker
*eekh bin dee-a-**bay**-teek-er*

I am allergic to penicillin
Ich bin auf Penizillin allergisch
*eekh bin owf pe-nee-tsee-**leen** a-**lerg**-eesh*

I am badly sunburnt
Ich habe einen starken Sonnenbrand
*eekh hab-e yn-en **shtark**-en **zon**-en-brant*

I am constipated
Ich habe Verstopfung
*eekh hab-e fer-**shtopf**-oong*

I cannot sleep
Ich kann nicht schlafen
*eekh kan neekht **shlaf**-en*

I feel dizzy
Ich fühle mich schwindelich
*eekh fûl-e meekh **shvinde**-leekh*

I feel faint
Ich fühle mich sehr schwach
*eekh fûl-e meekh zayr **shvakh***

I feel nauseous
Mir ist übel
*meer ist **ûb**-el*

I fell
Ich bin gefallen
*eekh bin ge-**fal**-en*

What's wrong?

I have a pain here
Ich habe hier Schmerzen
*eekh hab-e heer **shmerts**-en*

I have a rash here
Ich habe hier einen Ausschlag
*eekh hab-e heer yn-en **ows**-shlag*

I have been sick
Ich habe mich übergeben
*eekh hab-e meekh ûb-er-**gayb**-en*

I have been stung
Ich wurde gestochen
*eekh voord-e ge-**shtokh**-en*

I have cut myself
Ich habe mich geschnitten
*eekh hab-e meekh ge-**shnit**-en*

I have diarrhoea
Ich habe Durchfall
*eekh hab-e **doorkh**-fal*

I have pulled a muscle
Ich habe einen Muskel angerissen
*eekh hab-e yn-en **moosk**-el an-ge-ris-en*

I have sunstroke
Ich habe einen Sonnenstich
*eekh hab-e yn-en **zon**-en-shtikh*

I suffer from high blood pressure
Ich leide an hohem Blutdruck
*eekh **lyd**-e an **hoa**-em **bloot**-drook*

What's wrong?

I think I have food poisoning
Ich glaube ich habe eine Lebensmittelvergiftung
*eekh **glowb**-e eekh hab-e yn-e **layb**-enz-mit-el-fer-**gift**-oong*

It is inflamed here
Es ist hier entzündet
*es ist **heer** ent-tsûnd-et*

My arm is broken
Mein Arm ist gebrochen
*myn **arm** ist ge-**brokh**-en*

My stomach is upset
Ich habe einen verdorbenen Magen
*eekh hab-e yn-en fer-**dorb**-en-en **mag**-en*

My tongue is coated
Meine Zunge ist belegt
*myn-e **tsoong**-e ist be-**laygt***

She has a temperature
Sie hat erhöhte Temperatur
*zee hat er-**hoe**-te tem-pe-ra-**toor***

She has been bitten
Sie wurde gebissen
*zee voord-e ge-**bis**-en*

She has sprained her ankle
Sie hat sich den Knöchel verstaucht
*zee hat zeekh den **knoekh**-el fer-**shtowkht***

There is a swelling here
Da ist es geschwollen
*da ist es ge-**shvol**-en*

What's wrong?

I have hurt — my arm
   Ich habe — meinen Arm — verletzt
   *eekh hab-e — myn-en **arm** — fer-**letst***

            — my leg
            — mein Bein
            *— myn **byn***

            It is painful — to walk
   Ich habe Schmerzen beim — Gehen
   *eekh hab-e **shmerts-en** bym — **gay-en***

                — to breathe
                — Atmen
                *— **at-men***

                — to swallow
                — Schlucken
                *— **shlook-en***

I have — a headache
   Ich habe — Kopfschmerzen
   *eekh hab-e — **kopf-shmerts-en***

            — a sore throat
            — eine Halsentzündung
            *— yn-e **hals-ent-tsûnd-oong***

            — earache
            — Ohrenschmerzen
            *— **oar-en-shmerts-en***

            — cramp
            — einen Krampf
            *— yn-en **krampf***

What's wrong?

I am taking these drugs
Ich nehme diese Medikamente
*eekh **naym**-e deez-e may-dee-ka-**ment**-e*

Can you give me a prescription for them?
Können Sie mir ein Rezept dafür geben?
***koen**-en zee meer yn re-**tsept** da-fûr **gayb**-en*

Do I have to go into hospital?
Muß ich ins Krankenhaus gehen?
*moos eekh ins **krank**-en-hows **gay**-en*

Do I need an operation?
Brauche ich eine Operation?
browkh**-e eekh yn-e o-pe-ra-tsee-**oan

I am ill
Ich bin krank
*eekh bin **krank***

I am on the pill
Ich nehme die Pille
*eekh **naym**-e dee **pil**-e*

I am pregnant
Ich bin schwanger
*eekh bin **shvang**-er*

My blood group is...
Meine Blutgruppe ist...
*myn-e **bloot**-groop-e ist...*

I do not know my blood group
Ich kenne meine Blutgruppe nicht
*eekh **ken**-e myn-e **bloot**-groop-e **neekht***

At the hospital

Here is my E111 form
Hier ist mein E111.
*heer ist myn **ay**-hoond-ert-**elf***

How do I get reimbursed?
Wie bekomme ich die Kosten zurückerstattet?
***vee** be-kom-e eekh dee **kost**-en tsoo-**rûk**-er-shtat-et*

Must I stay in bed?
Muß ich im Bett bleiben?
***moos** eekh im **bet** blyb-en*

When will I be able to travel?
Wann werde ich in der Lage sein, zu reisen?
***van** vayrd-e eekh in der **lag**-e zyn tsoo **ryz**-en*

Will I be able to go out tomorrow?
Werde ich morgen das Haus verlassen können?
*vayrd-e eekh **morg**-en das **hows** ver-**lass**-en koen-en*

Parts of the body

ankle
Fußgelenk
***foos**-ge-lenk*

arm
Arm
arm

back
Rücken
***rûk**-en*

bone
Knochen
***knokh**-en*

Parts of the body

breast
Brust
broost

cheek
Wange
vang-e

chest
Brust
broost

ear
Ohr
oar

elbow
Ellbogen
el-boag-en

eye
Auge
owg-e

face
Gesicht
ge-zeekht

finger
Finger
fing-er

foot
Fuß
foos

hand
Hand
hant

heart
Herz
herts

kidney
Niere
neer-e

knee
Knie
knee

leg
Bein
byn

liver
Leber
layb-er

lungs
Lunge
loong-e

mouth
Mund
moont

muscle
Muskel
moosk-el

Parts of the body

neck
Hals
hals

stomach
Magen
mag-en

nose
Nase
naz-e

throat
Hals
hals

skin
Haut
howt

wrist
Handgelenk
hant-ge-lenk

At the dentist's

I have toothache
Ich habe Zahnschmerzen
eekh hab-e tsan-shmerts-en

I have broken a tooth
Ich habe einen zerbrochenen Zahn
eekh hab-e yn-en tser-brokh-en-en tsan

I have to see the dentist
Ich muß zum Zahnarzt gehen
eekh moos tsoom tsan-artst gay-en

My false teeth are broken
Meine dritten Zähne sind kaputt
myn-e drit-en tsen-e zint ka-poot

Can you repair them?
Können Sie sie reparieren?
koen-en zee zee re-ar-reer-en

At the dentist's

My gums are sore
Mein Zahnfleisch ist entzündet
myn tsan-flysh ist ent-tsûnd-et

Please give me an injection
Geben Sie mir bitte eine Spritze
gayb-en zee meer bit-e yn-e shprits-e

That hurts
Das tut weh
das toot vay

The filling has come out
Die Plombe ist herausgefallen
dee blomb-e ist hayr-ows-ge-fal-en

This one hurts
Der tut weh
dayr toot vay

Are you going to fill it?
Werden Sie ihn füllen?
vayrd-en zee een fûl-en

Will you have to take it out?
Müssen Sie ihn ziehen?
mûs-en zee een tsee-en

FOR YOUR INFORMATION

Numbers

0	null	*nool*
1	eins	*yns*
2	zwei	*tsvy*
3	drei	*dry*
4	vier	*feer*
5	fünf	*fûnf*
6	sechs	*zeks*
7	sieben	*zeeb-en*
8	acht	*akht*
9	neun	*noyn*
10	zehn	*tsayn*
11	elf	*elf*
12	zwölf	*tsvoelf*
13	dreizehn	*dry-tsayn*
14	vierzehn	*feer-tsayn*
15	fünfzehn	*fûnf-tsayn*
16	sechzehn	*zekhs-tsayn*
17	siebzehn	*zeeb-tsayn*
18	achtzehn	*akht-tsayn*

Numbers

19	neunzehn *noyn*-stayn
20	zwanzig *tsvan-tseekh*
21	einundzwanzig *yn*-oont-tsvan-tseekh
22	zweiundzwanzig *tsvy*-oont-tsvan-tseekh
23	dreiundzwanzig *dry*-oont-tsvan-tseekh
24	vierundzwanzig *feer*-oont-tsvan-steekh
25	fünfundzwanzig *fûnf*-oont-tsvan-tseekh
26	sechsundzwanzig *zeks*-oont-tsvan-tseekh
27	siebenundzwanzig *zeeb*-en-oont-tsvan-steekh
28	achtundzwanzig *akht*-oont-tsvan-tseekh
29	neunundzwanzig *noyn*-oont-tsvan-tseekh
30	dreißig *dry-seekh*
40	vierzig *feer-tseekh*
50	fünfzig *fûnf-tseekh*
60	sechzig *zekh-tseekh*
70	siebzig *zeeb-tseekh*
80	achtzig *akh-tseekh*
90	neunzig *noyn-tseekh*
100	hundert *hoond-ert*
200	zweihundert *tsvy-hoond-ert*
300	dreihundert *dry-hoond-ert*

Numbers

400	vierhundert *feer-hoond-ert*
500	fünfhundert *fûnf-hoond-ert*
600	sechshundert *zeks-hoond-ert*
700	siebenhundert *zeeb-en-hoond-ert*
800	achthundert *akht-hoond-ert*
900	neunhundert *noyn-hoond-ert*
1000	tausend *towz-ent*
2000	zweitausend *tsvy-towz-ent*
3000	dreitausen *dry-towz-ent*
4000	viertausend *feer-towz-ent*
1000000	eine Million *yn-e mee-lee-oan*

Ordinals

1st	erster *erst-er*
2nd	zweiter *tsvyt-er*
3rd	dritter *drit-er*
4th	vierter *feert-er*
5th	fünfter *fûnft-er*
xth	xter *xt-er*

Fractions and percentages

a half	ein halb *yn halp*
a quarter	ein Viertel *yn feert-el*
a third	ein Drittel *yn drit-el*
two thirds	zwei Drittel *tsvy drit-el*
10%	zehn Prozent *tsayn pro-tsent*

Days

Sunday	Sonntag *zon-tag*
Monday	Montag *moan-tag*
Tuesday	Dienstag *deens-tag*
Wednesday	Mittwoch *mit-vokh*
Thursday	Donnerstag *don-ers-tag*
Friday	Freitag *fry-tag*
Saturday	Samstag *zams-tag*

Dates

on Friday	am Freitag *am fry-tag*
next Tuesday	nächsten Dienstag *nekst-en **deens**-tag*
last Tuesday	letzten Dienstag *letst-en **deens**-tag*
yesterday	gestern ***gest**-ern*
today	heute ***hoyt**-e*
tomorrow	morgen ***morg**-en*
in June	im Juni *im **yoon**-ee*
7th July	siebter Juli ***zeept**-er **yool**-ee*
next week	nächste Woche *nekst-e **vokh**-e*
last month	letzten Monat *letst-en **moa**-nat*

The Seasons

spring	Frühjahr ***frû**-yar*
summer	Sommer ***zom**-er*
autumn	Herbst *herpst*
winter	Winter ***vint**-er*

Times of the year

in spring	im Frühjahr *im frû-yar*
in summer	im Sommer *im zom-er*
in autumn	im Herbst *im herpst*
in winter	im Winter *im vint-er*

Months

January	Januar *ya-noo-ar*
February	Februar *fayb-roo-ar*
March	März *merts*
April	April *a-preel*
May	Mai *my*
June	Juni *yoon-ee*
July	Juli *yool-ee*
August	August *ow-goost*
September	September *zep-temb-er*
October	Oktober *ok-toab-er*
November	November *noa-vemb-er*
December	Dezember *day-tsemb-er*

Public holidays

Public holidays

1st January, New Year's Day
Neujahr
noy-yar

6th January, Twelfth Night
Heilige Dreikönige
hyl-eege dry-koen-eege

Good Friday
Karfreitag
kar-fry-tag

Easter Sunday
Ostersonntag
oast-er-zon-tag

Easter Monday
Ostermontag
oast-er-moan-tag

1st May, May Day
Maifeiertag
my-fy-er-tag

Ascension
Christi Himmelfahrt
krist-ee him-el-fart

Whit Sunday
Pfingstsonntag
pfingst-zon-tag

Public holidays

Whit Monday
Pfingstmontag
*pfingst-**moan**-tag*

Corpus Christi
Fronleichnam
*fron-**lykh**-nam*

Feast of the Assumption
Maria Himmelfahrt (Catholic regions)
*ma-**ree**-a **him**-el-fart*

3 October, German unification
Tag der Einheit
tag *der **yn**-hyt*

1 November, All Saints' Day
Allerheiligen
*al-er-**hyl**-eeg-en*

24th December, Christmas Eve
Heilig Abend (shops closed in afternoon)
***hyl**-eekh **a**-bent*

25th December, Christmas Day
erster Weihnachtsfeiertag
***erst**-er **vy**-nakhts-fy-er-tag*

26th December, Boxing Day
zweiter Weihnachtsfeiertag
***tsvyt**-er **vy**-nakhts-fy-er-tag*

31st December, New Year's Eve
Sylvester
*zil-**vest**-er*

Colours

Colours

beige
beige
bayzh

black
schwarz
shvarts

blue
blau
blow

brown
braun
brown

cream
cremefarben
kraym-farb-en

fawn
khaki
ka-kee

gold
golden
gold-en

green
grün
grûn

grey
grau
grow

mauve
violett
vee-oa-let

orange
orange
o-ranzh-e

pink
rosa
roaz-a

purple
lila
lee-la

red
rot
roat

silver
silbern
zilb-ern

tan
gelbbraun
gelp-brown

Common adjectives

white
weiß
vys

yellow
gelb
gelp

Common adjectives

bad
schlecht
shlekht

beautiful
schön
shoen

big
groß
groas

cheap
billig
beel-eekh

cold
kalt
kalt

expensive
teuer
toy-er

difficult
schwierig
shveer-eekh

easy
leicht
lykht

fast
schnell
shnel

good
gut
goot

high
hoch
hoakh

hot
heiß
hys

little
wenig
vayn-eekh

long
lang
lang

Common adjectives

new
neu
noy

old
alt
alt

short
kurz
koorts

slow
langsam
lang-zam

small
klein
klyn

ugly
häßlich
hes-leekh

Signs and notices

Achtung
akh-toong
caution

Aufzug
owf-tsoog
lift/elevator

Ausgang
ows-gang
exit

Information
in-for-ma-tsee-oan
information

Ausverkauf
ows-fer-kowf
sale

Verkauft
fer-kowft
sold out

besetzt
be-zetst
occupied

nicht auf das Gras gehen
*neekht owf das **gras** gay-en*
keep off the grass

bitte klingeln
*bit-e **kling**-eln*
please ring

drücken
drûk-en
push

Eingang
yn-gang
entrance

Eintritt frei
*yn-trit **fry***
no admission charge

Telefon
tay-lay-foan
telephone

Feuerwehr
foy-er-vayr
fire brigade

frei
fry
vacant

Fundamt
foont-amt
Lost Property Office

Signs and notices

Betreten verboten
be-trayt-en fer-boat-en
No trespassing

Gefahr
ge-far
danger

geschlossen
ge-shlos-en
closed

Gift
gift
poison

heiß
hys
hot

kalt
kalt
cold

Kasse
kas-e
cashier

Durchfahrt verboten
doorkh-fart fer-boat-en
no thoroughfare

kein Eingang
kyn yn-gang
no entry

Krankenhaus
krank-en-hows
hospital

Sanitäter
zan-ee-tet-er
ambulance

Lebensgefahr
layb-ens-ge-far
danger of death

Nachmittags geschlossen
nakh-mit-ags-ge-shlos-en
closed in the afternoon

nicht berühren
neekht be-rûr-en
do not touch

nicht nach außen lehnen
neekht nakh ows-en layn-en
do not lean out

Rauchen verboten
rowkh-en fer-boat-en
no smoking

Notausgang
noat-ows-gang
emergency exit

private Zufahrt
pree-vat-e tsoo-fart
private road

Signs and notices

Radweg
rat-vayg
cycle path

Raucherabteil
rowkh-er-ap-tyl
smoking compartment

Geschäftsauflösung
ge-shefts-owf-loez-oong
closing down sale

bitte rechts fahren
bit-e rekhts far-en
keep to the right

Andenken
an-denk-en
souvenirs

Reiseagentur
ryz-e-a-gen-toor
travel agency

Sonderangebot
zond-er-an-ge-boat
special offer

Trinkwasser
trink-vas-er
drinking water

Umleitung
oom-lyt-oong
diversion

ziehen
tsee-en
pull

zu verkaufen
tsoo-fer-kowf-en
for sale

zu mieten
tsoo meet-en
to let/for hire

Preisliste
prys-list-e
price list

willkommen
vil-kom-en
welcome

Gepäck
*ge-**pek***
baggage

Bank
bank
bank

Zoll
tsol
Customs

Notfall
***noat**-fal*
Emergency

Signs and notices

Feuermelder
foy-er-meld-er
fire alarm

reserviert
re-zer-veert
reserved

Raucherbereich
rowkh-er-be-rykh
smoking area

nur für — erlaubt
noor für — er-lowpt
allowed only for —

Achtung vor dem Hund
akh-toong foar dem hoont
beware of the dog

Polizei
po-lee-tsy
police

Feuergefahr
foy-er-ge-far
danger of fire

Nur für Mitarbeiter
noor für mit-ar-byt-er
employees only

Abfahrt/Abflüge
ap-fart/ap-flug-e
departures

Abfall
ap-fal
litter

offen
of-en
open

klingeln
kling-eln
ring

Ankunft
an-koonft
arrivals

Schule
shool-e
school

Eingang
yn-gang
entrance

Zeitplan
tstyt-plan
timetable

Herren
her-en
gentlemen

Damen
dam-en
ladies

Signs and notices

Fotografieren verboten
foa-toa-gra-feer-en fer-boat-en
no picture taking

Notbremse
noat-bremz-e
communication cord (rail)

nur zur äußerlichen Anwendung
noor tsoor oys-er-leekh-en an-vend-oong
for external use only

Es ist verboten, während der Fahrt mit dem Fahrer zu sprechen
es ist fer-boat-en ver-ent der fart mit dem far-er tsoo shprekh-en
It is forbidden to speak to the driver while the bus is moving

eintreten, ohne zu klopfen
yn-trayt-en oan-e tsoo klopf-en
enter without knocking

Parken nur für Anwohner
park-en noor für an-voan-er
parking for residents only

IN AN EMERGENCY

Call — the fire brigade
Rufen — Sie die Feuerwehr
roof-en — zee dee foy-er-vayr

— the police
— Sie die Polizei
— zee dee po-lee-tsy

— an ambulance
— Sie die Sanitäter
— zee dee zan-ee-tet-er

Get a doctor
Holen Sie einen Arzt
hoal-en zee yn-en artst

There is a fire
Es brennt
es brent

Where is — the police station?
Wo ist — die Polizeiwache?
voa ist — dee po-lee-tsy-vakh-e

— the British consulate?
— das britische Konsulat?
— das bri-tish-e koan-soo-lat